How To Use This Study Guide

This five-lesson study guide corresponds to *"Getting the Basics Right" With Rick Renner* (Renner TV). Each lesson in this study guide covers a topic that is addressed during the program series, with questions and references supplied to draw you deeper into your own private study of the Scriptures on this subject.

To derive the most benefit from this study guide, consider the following:

First, watch or listen to the program prior to working through the corresponding lesson in this guide. (Programs can also be viewed at **renner.org** by clicking on the Media/Archives links or on our Renner Ministries YouTube channel.)

Second, take the time to look up the scriptures included in each lesson. Prayerfully consider their application to your own life.

Third, use a journal or notebook to make note of your answers to each lesson's Study Questions and Practical Application challenges.

Fourth, invest specific time in prayer and in the Word of God to consult with the Holy Spirit. Write down the scriptures or insights He reveals to you.

Finally, take action! Whatever the Lord tells you to do according to His Word, do it.

For added insights on this subject, it is recommended that you obtain Rick Renner's book *Signs You'll See Just Before Jesus Comes*. You may also select from Rick's other available resources by placing your order at **renner.org** or by calling 1-800-742-5593.

LESSON 1

TOPIC
Right and Wrong Dealings With Money

SCRIPTURES
1. **1 Timothy 6:10** — For the love of money is the root of all evil....
2. **James 5:1-6** — Go to now, ye rich men, weep and howl for your miseries that shall come upon you. Your riches are corrupted, and your garments are motheaten. Your gold and silver is cankered; and the rust of them shall be a witness against you, and shall eat your flesh as it were fire. Ye have heaped treasure together for the last days. Behold, the hire of the labourers who have reaped down your fields, which is of you kept back by fraud, crieth: and the cries of them which have reaped are entered into the ears of the Lord of sabaoth. Ye have lived in pleasure on the earth, and been wanton; ye have nourished your hearts, as in a day of slaughter. Ye have condemned and killed the just; and he doth not resist you.
3. **Genesis 4:10** — And he said, What hast thou done? the voice of thy brother's blood crieth unto me from the ground.
4. **Genesis 18:20,21** — And the Lord said, Because the cry of Sodom and Gomorrah is great, and because their sin is very grievous; I will go down now, and see whether they have done altogether according to the cry of it, which is come unto me; and if not, I will know.
5. **Exodus 3:7** — And the Lord said, I have surely seen the affliction of my people which are in Egypt, and have heard their cry by reason of their taskmasters; for I know their sorrows.

GREEK WORDS
1. "go to now" — Ἄγε νῦν (*age nun*): let me help lead you, now
2. "rich men" — πλούσιος (*plousios*): vast wealth; extreme riches; incredible abundance; used by Plato to say no one was richer than legendary King Midas
3. "weep" — κλαίω (*klaio*): to weep; to wail; to shed tears; to sob

A Note From Rick Renner

I am on a personal quest to see a "revival of the Bible" so people can establish their lives on a firm foundation that will stand strong and endure the test as end-time storm winds begin to intensify.

In order to experience a revival of the Bible in your personal life, it is important to take time each day to read, receive, and apply its truths to your life. James tells us that if we will continue in the perfect law of liberty — refusing to be forgetful hearers, but determined to be doers — we will be blessed in our ways. As you watch or listen to the programs in this series and work through this corresponding study guide, I trust you will search the Scriptures and allow the Holy Spirit to help you hear something new from God's Word that applies specifically to your life. I encourage you to be a doer of the Word He reveals to you. Whatever the cost, I assure you — it will be worth it.

> Thy words were found, and I did eat them;
> and thy word was unto me the joy and rejoicing of mine heart:
> for I am called by thy name, O Lord God of hosts.
> — Jeremiah 15:16

Your brother and friend in Jesus Christ,

Rick Renner

Unless otherwise indicated, all scripture quotations are taken from the *King James Version* of the Bible.

Scripture quotations marked (*AMPC*) are taken from the *Amplified® Bible*. Copyright © 1954, 1958, 1962, 1964, 1965, 1987 by The Lockman Foundation. Used by permission. **www.Lockman.org**.

Scripture quotations marked (*NKJV*) are taken from the *New King James Version®*. Copyright © 1982 by Thomas Nelson. Used by permission. All rights reserved.

Scripture quotations marked (*NIV*) are taken from Holy Bible, New International Version®, *NIV*® Copyright ©1973, 1978, 1984, 2011 by Biblica, Inc.® Used by permission. All rights reserved worldwide.

Getting the Basics Right

Copyright © 2022 by Rick Renner
P.O. Box 702040
Tulsa, OK 74170

Published by Rick Renner Ministries
www.renner.org

ISBN 13: 978-1-6803-1996-5

eBook ISBN 13: 978-1-6803-1997-2

All rights reserved. No portion of this book may be reproduced or transmitted in any form or by any means — electronic, mechanical, photocopy, recording, scanning, or other — except for brief quotations in critical reviews or articles, without the prior written permission of the Publisher.

4. "howl" — ὀλολύζω (*ololudzo*): to bewail, cry, or lament; to express feelings too deep for words; to wail
5. "miseries" — ταλαιπωρία (*talaiporia*): calloused condition; insensitive condition; a miserable condition
6. "upon" — ἐπὶ (*epi*): upon; as to cover
7. "your riches" — ὁ πλοῦτος ὑμῶν (*ho ploutos humon*): a definite article with πλοῦτος (*ploutos*); THE riches of yours; THE riches you have accumulated; the definite article points explicitly to the riches accumulated by this particular category of person
8. "corrupted" — σήπω (*sepo*): have become rotten; origins of the word sepsis, a life-threatening infection that triggers a chain reaction throughout the body and that, without treatment, can rapidly lead to tissue damage, organ failure, and death
9. "garments" — ἱμάτιον (*himation*): plural; the exquisite, brightly colored, beaded, posh, outer garment that was popular among rich Greeks and Romans in the First Century; a sign of status and wealth
10. "motheaten" — σητόβρωτος (*setobrotos*): eaten or devoured by moths
11. "gold" — ὁ χρυσὸς ὑμῶν (*ho chrusos humon*): a definite article with χρυσός (*chrusos*), gold; the most valuable material that existed in the ancient world; here, THE gold of yours; THE gold you have accumulated; not referring to all gold, but to THE gold of this particular person or group of people
12. "silver" — ὁ ἄργυρος (*ho arguros*): a definite article with ἄργυρος (*arguros*), silver; a word that often referred to money because silver was the primary metal used for coins; here, THE silver or money of yours; THE silver or money you have accumulated; not referring to all silver or money, but to THE silver or money of this particular person or group of people
13. "witness" — μαρτύριον (*marturion*): from μάρτυς (*martus*), one summoned to testify in a court of law; first-hand testimony and evidence presented in a legal case in a court of law
14. "against" — εἰς (*eis*): to enter; to be admitted
15. "eat" — φάγω (*phago*): here, will eat; will consume; will devour
16. "your flesh" — τὰς σάρκας ὑμῶν (*tas sarkas humon*): literally, the flesh of you; the flesh of the particular category of person he is referring to in this verse
17. "as" — ὡς (*hos*): just as; similar to

18. "fire" — **πῦρ** (*pur*): burning fire with its twisting, swirling, whirling, flickering flames that bend, twist, turn, and arch upward; here, fire is pictured burning flesh
19. "heaped treasure together" — **Θησαυρίζω** (*thesauridzo*): from **Θησαυρός** (*thesaurus*), a treasure, a treasure chamber, or a place of safekeeping where riches and fortunes are kept; does not refer to every person who has accumulated money, but applies to the person or category of people he is referring to in the passage
20. "last days" — **ἐσχάταις ἡμέραις** (*eschatais hemerais*): from **ἔσχατος** (*eschatos*) and **ἡμέρα** (*hemera*); the word **ἔσχατος** (*eschatos*) points to the ultimate end of a thing like the final port or last stopping off point for a long journey; the word **ἡμέρα** (*hemera*) is plural in this verse, hence, it means days; it may point to the last part of a person's journey on earth, the end of their life, or their senior years; the phrase **ἐσχάταις ἡμέραις** (*eschatais hemerais*) could point to the last days in terms of eschatology
21. "behold" — **ἰδού** (*idou*): bewilderment, shock, amazement, and wonder
22. "hire" — **ὁ μισθὸς** (*ho misthos*): a definite article with **μισθὸς** (*misthos*); the word **μισθὸς** (*misthos*) means pay, salary, or reward, and refers to compensation for one's work; here, however, with a definite article, meaning THE salaries, THE wages, THE compensation; it is not all wages, but the incorrect wages that are paid by this particular kind of employer
23. "labourers" — **ἐργάτης** (*ergates*): a workman; a laborer; an employee
24. "reaped down your fields" — **ἀμησάντων τὰς χώρας ὑμῶν** (*amesanton tas choras humon*): the word **ὑμῶν** (*humon*) means of yours and points to the fact that these words are not directed to everyone, but to a particular category of employers and landowners
25. "of you kept back" — **ὁ ἀφυστερημένος ἀφ' ὑμῶν** (*ho aphustermenos aph' humon*): to deprive, to keep back, to cheat, defraud, or rob what rightfully belongs to someone else; the word **ὑμῶν** (*humon*) means of yours and points to the fact that these words are not directed to everyone, but to a particular category of employers and landowners
26. "crieth" — **κράζω** (*kradzo*): to scream, yell, exclaim, or cry out at the top of one's voice; to shriek; an urgent shout; a loud outburst of emotion
27. "Lord Sabaoth" — **Κυρίου Σαβαὼθ** (*Kuriou Sabaoth*): the word **σαβαώθ** depicts an army or host; an innumerable throng or limitless

army; correlates to the phrase "the Lord of hosts" in the Old Testament and pictures the Lord organizing for war and crushing and going forth to militarily crush an enemy

28. "lived in pleasure" — τρυφάω (*truphao*): a luxurious life; to live self-indulgently
29. "wanton" — σπαταλάω (*spatalao*): to live extravagantly; to indulge in luxury; to live wastefully; to live with no indulgent restrictions; lewd living
30. "nourished" — τρέφω (*trepho*): nourished; fed; fatten; enlarged
31. "your hearts" — τὰς καρδίας ὑμῶν (*tas kardias humon*): literally, the hearts of you; not referring to everyone, but to this particular category of individuals
32. "killed" — φονεύω (*phoneuo*): kill; murder; commit homicide; intentional murder; slaughter
33. "the just" — τὸν δίκαιον (*ton dikaion*): a definite article with δίκαιος (*dikaios*); THE just; THE upright; THE ones who have done right and are right in the sight of God
34. "not" — οὐκ (*ouk*): an emphatic not
35. "resist" — ἀντιτάσσομαι (*antitassomai*): to stand against; to set one's self against

SYNOPSIS

The five lessons in this study on ***Getting the Basics Right*** will focus on the following topics:

- Right and Wrong Dealings With Money
- The Lord Is Coming Soon
- Let Your 'Yea Be Yea' and Your 'Nay Be Nay'
- Praying for Each Other
- Hiding a Multitude of Sins

The emphasis of this lesson:

**A significant number of extremely rich employers were not compensating their workers correctly, and James called them out for it. They had become self-absorbed, calloused, and insensitive to the needs of their workers, and as a result, their wealth became disease-ridden and testified against them. If you're employed and feel that you're not being paid fairly, know that God hears your cries for justice and will set the record straight in due time.

In First Timothy 6:10, the apostle Paul issues a strong warning to all believers regarding money. He said, "For the love of money is the root of all evil…." Money, in and of itself, is not evil, but when we become so driven to have it and hoard it, and we're afraid of losing it, we're out of balance and heading for problems.

James also wrote about money in his letter to First-Century believers who had been scattered abroad all across the eastern lands of the Mediterranean Sea. As a result of Roman persecution, countless Christians had been evicted from their homes, separated from their family members, terminated from their jobs, and forced into low-level positions that paid very little.

This issue of financial compensation is the focus of **James 5:1-6**, where James wrote:

> **Go to now, ye rich men, weep and howl for your miseries that shall come upon you.**
>
> **Your riches are corrupted, and your garments are motheaten.**
>
> **Your gold and silver is cankered; and the rust of them shall be a witness against you, and shall eat your flesh as it were fire. Ye have heaped treasure together for the last days.**
>
> **Behold, the hire of the labourers who have reaped down your fields, which is of you kept back by fraud, crieth: and the cries of them which have reaped are entered into the ears of the Lord of sabaoth.**
>
> **Ye have lived in pleasure on the earth, and been wanton; ye have nourished your hearts, as in a day of slaughter.**
>
> **Ye have condemned and killed the just; and he doth not resist you.**

As we carefully read through these first six verses of James 5, we can clearly see that employers were not treating their employees fairly. To effectively unpack the meaning of this passage, let's examine the original Greek meanings of several key words in each verse.

A Word of Warning to Extravagantly Rich Employers

To address the issue of fair and accurate compensation for workers, James begins in verse 1 by saying:

> Go to now, ye rich men, weep and howl for your miseries that shall come upon you.
> —James 5:1

The phrase "go to now" in Greek is *age nun*, which means *let me help lead you, now*. This subject of finances is so very important, James said, "Hey, let me lead you right now on this issue." Specifically, he addressed "rich men," which is a translation of the Greek word *plousios*, describing *vast wealth*; *extreme riches*; or *incredible abundance*. This word was used by Plato to describe the legendary wealth of King Midas.

James' use of the word *plousios* lets us know he is talking about *extremely wealthy individuals*. It is to this group of people he said, "Weep and howl." In Greek, the word "weep" is *klaio*, which means *to weep*; *to wail*; *to shed tears*; or *to sob*. The word "howl" is the Greek word *ololudzo*, and it means *to bewail, cry, or lament*. It expresses *feelings too deep for words* and depicts *one that is wailing uncontrollably*.

Why did James admonish the extremely rich to *weep* and *howl*? He said it was on account of "…your miseries that shall come upon you" (James 5:1). The Greek word for "miseries" here is *talaiporia*, and it describes *a person who is in a calloused condition* and *totally insensitive to the needs of others*. Consequently, they are in a *miserable* condition. To the exceedingly rich employers who were insensitive to the needs of their employees, James said that something was going to come "upon" them, which literally means *something is about to come right on top of you and cover you*.

Treating Workers Unfairly Produces Septic-like Conditions

James went on to say, "Your riches are corrupted, and your garments are motheaten" (James 5:2). What's interesting about this verse is that when you read it in the Greek, the phrase "your riches" — which is *ho ploutos humon* — literally says *THE riches of yours* or *THE riches you have accumulated*. It is a definite article with the word *ploutos*, and the definite article points explicitly to the riches accumulated by this particular category of person.

To be clear, James is *not* addressing all rich people. He's addressing the extravagantly wealthy individuals who financially abuse those who work for them. These are employers who do not financially compensate their workers correctly. That is why their riches are "corrupted."

In Greek, the word "corrupted" here is *sepo*, which means *has become rotten*. This word *sepo* is the origin of our modern word *sepsis*, which is a life-threatening infection that triggers a chain reaction throughout the body and, without treatment, can rapidly lead to tissue damage, organ failure, and death. The use of this word *sepo* — translated here as "corrupted" — tells us that when someone hires a person to do a job and they fail to pay them a fair wage, it releases a *septic-like infection*. It is a toxicity that triggers a chain reaction of corruption and calamity in their lives.

James specifically told these unfair landowners, "…Your garments are motheaten" (James 5:2). The word "garments" is *himation* in Greek, and it describes *the exquisite, brightly colored, beaded, posh, outer garments that were popular among rich Greeks and Romans in the First Century*. This extravagant attire was a sign of status and wealth. Those who decked themselves in such opulent apparel but treated their workers poorly would find their clothing "motheaten," translated from the Greek word *setobrotos*, which means *eaten or devoured by moths*.

The Riches of the Corrupt Will Testify Against Them

Not only would the clothes of the ruthlessly rich become tattered, but also their money itself. James said, "Your gold and silver is cankered; and the rust of them shall be a witness against you, and shall eat your flesh as it were fire. Ye have heaped treasure together for the last days" (James 5:3).

The words "your gold" in this verse are a rendering of the Greek phrase *ho chrusos humon*. It contains a definite article, which means it could literally be translated *THE gold of yours* or *THE gold you have accumulated*. The word *chrusos* is the term for *gold*, and it signifies *the most valuable material that existed in the ancient world*. The fact that James included the definite article tells us he is not referring to all gold, but to THE gold of this particular person or group of people.

Likewise, their "silver" would be affected. In Greek, "silver" is *ho arguros*, which again contains a definite article — this time with the word *arguros*, the term for *silver*. Interestingly, *arguros* is a word that often referred to *money of any kind* because silver was the primary metal used for coins. Here, it literally means *THE silver or money of yours* or *THE silver or money you have accumulated*. Again, as with THE gold, this was not referring to all silver or money, but to THE silver or money of this particular person or group of people.

To the lavishly wealthy employers who treated their workers wrongly, James said, "Your gold and silver is cankered; and the rust of them shall be a witness against you..." (James 5:3). The word "witness" in Greek is *marturion*, from the Greek word *martus*, and it describes *one summoned to testify in a court of law*. It is *first-hand testimony and evidence presented in a legal case in a court of law*.

Thus, James said the gold and silver of these dishonorable employers would be summoned to the witness stand to give first-hand testimony *against* their unscrupulous actions. This word "against" is the Greek word *eis*, which means *to enter* or *to be admitted*. The testimony provided by the wealth of the corrupt businessmen would be admitted as evidence in the courts of Heaven.

The Wealth They've Stockpiled for Their Senior Years Will End Up Burning Them Just Like Fire

James continued by saying, "...[It] shall eat your flesh as it were fire..." (James 5:3). The word "eat" here is the Greek term *phago*, meaning *will eat; will consume;* or *will devour*. "Your flesh" in Greek is *tas sarkas humon*, which literally means *the flesh of you* and refers to the flesh of the particular category of person he is referring to in this verse.

Again, James is not talking about every wealthy employer — just the rich employers who abuse their positions and don't correctly compensate their workers. He said their riches would devour their flesh "as it were fire." The word "as" in Greek is the word *hos*, which means *just as* or *similar to*. The Greek word for "fire" is *pur*, and it signifies *burning fire with its twisting, swirling, whirling, flickering flames that bend, twist, turn, and arch upward*. Here, fire is pictured burning flesh. This is a very sobering warning to those who fail to pay their workers fairly.

At this point, James added, "...Ye have heaped treasure together for the last days" (James 5:3). The phrase "heaped treasure together" is a translation of the Greek word *thesauridzo*, from the word *thesaurus*, which is *a treasure, a treasure chamber,* or *a place of safekeeping where riches and fortunes are kept*. Again, this does not refer to every person who has accumulated money, but it applies to the person or category of people James is referring to in this passage — those who have great wealth and could have treated their workers better but didn't.

This brings us to the phrase "last days," which in Greek is *eschatais hemerais*, from the words *eschatos* and *hemera*. The word *eschatos* points to *the ultimate end of a thing like the final port or last stopping off point for a long journey*. The word *hemera* is plural in this verse, hence, it means *days*; it may point to *the last part of a person's journey on earth, the end of their life,* or *their senior years*. When these words are joined together, the phrase *eschatais hemerais* — "last days" — could point to *the last days in terms of eschatology*.

The implication here in James' letter is that he's writing to very wealthy people who are accumulating and stockpiling wealth in order to make sure they will be well taken care of in *the senior years of their life*. The problem is that they are not correctly compensating people for the services they are providing, which is shameful in God's eyes.

Certain Prosperous Landowners Were Cheating and Withholding Finances From Their Workers

When we come to James 5:4, he added even more details to the description of what these rich yet stingy people were doing:

> **Behold, the hire of the labourers who have reaped down your fields, which is of you kept back by fraud, crieth: and the cries of them which have reaped are entered into the ears of the Lord of sabaoth.**

Notice the first word "behold." It is the Greek word *idou*, and it carries the idea of *bewilderment, shock, amazement,* and *wonder*. It is the equivalent of James saying, "Wow! It is amazing and shocking what you're doing...." He then pointed specifically to "...the hire of the labourers who have reaped down your fields..." (James 5:4).

The word "hire" in Greek is *ho misthos*, which again contains a definite article (*ho*) along with *misthos*. The word *misthos* describes *pay, salary,* or *reward*, and refers to *compensation for one's work*. Here, however, with a definite article, it means *THE salaries, THE wages,* or *THE compensation*. It is not all wages and compensation, but *the incorrect wages that are paid* by this particular kind of employer.

The word "labourers" is the Greek word *ergates*, which describes *a workman, a laborer,* or *an employee*. Particularly, James calls attention to the workers that "reaped down your fields," which in Greek is *amesanton tas choras humon*. Again, we see the word *humon*, which means *of yours* and would better be translated here as *the fields of you*. The use of this definite article clearly indicates that these words are not directed to everyone, but to a particular category of employers and landowners.

James described the fields as "…which is of you kept back by fraud…" (James 5:4). The phrase "of you kept back" means *to deprive, to keep back, to cheat, defraud,* or *rob what rightfully belongs to someone else*. Once again, the Greek text of this phrase includes the word *humon*, which means *of yours* and points to the fact that these words are not directed to everyone, but to a particular category of employers and landowners — those who are not correctly compensating their workers.

The workers who had been cheated of what was rightfully theirs "…crieth: and the cries of them which have reaped are entered into the ears of the Lord of sabaoth" (James 5:4). The word "crieth" here is the Greek word *kradzo*, which means *to scream, yell, exclaim,* or *cry out at the top of one's voice*. It is *a shriek, an urgent shout,* or *a loud outburst of emotion* that erupts through the atmosphere and makes it all the way into the ears of the Lord Himself.

God Hears Our Cries

When we study the Scripture, we see that there are certain things that happen on earth that make it directly to the ears of God. For example, God hears *the cry of innocent blood* that has been shed. When Cain killed his brother Able, the Bible says:

> **And he [God] said, What hast thou done? the voice of thy brother's blood crieth unto me from the ground.**
> **— Genesis 4:10**

Not only does God hear the cry of blood that's been shed, but also *the sound of sin*. During Abraham's day, the sin of the people living in the cities of Sodom and Gomorrah was exceedingly dreadful. In fact, it was so appalling the Bible says:

> And the Lord said, Because the cry of Sodom and Gomorrah is great, and because their sin is very grievous; I will go down now, and see whether they have done altogether according to the cry of it, which is come unto me; and if not, I will know.
> — Genesis 18:20,21

Something else that makes it directly into the ears of God is *the cry of injustice*. When the nation of Israel — God's chosen people — had been in bondage and treated harshly for many years, the Bible says:

> And the Lord said, I have surely seen the affliction of my people which are in Egypt, and have heard their cry by reason of their taskmasters; for I know their sorrows.
> — Exodus 3:7

Make no mistake: Nothing is hidden from God's sight. Scripture says, "…All things are naked and open to the eyes of Him to whom we must give account" (Hebrews 4:13 *NKJV*). This is why James cautioned employers, "Behold, the hire of the labourers who have reaped down your fields, which is of you kept back by fraud, crieth: and *the cries of them which have reaped are entered into the ears of the Lord of sabaoth*" (James 5:4).

When people are not being paid fairly, their cries of injustice reach the ears of the "Lord Sabaoth." The Greek rendering of this title is *Kuriou Sabaoth*. The word *Sabaoth* depicts *an army or host; an innumerable throng or limitless army*. It correlates to the phrase "the Lord of hosts" in the Old Testament and pictures the Lord organizing for war and crushing and going forth to militarily crush an enemy. This tells us that the Lord will mobilize His forces to answer the cries of those being financially robbed of what is rightfully theirs.

Corrupt Employers Live Wasteful, Self-indulgent Lives

What else does James say about these unscrupulous employers? He goes on to say:

> Ye have lived in pleasure on the earth, and been wanton; ye have nourished your hearts, as in a day of slaughter.
> —James 5:5

Notice the phrase "lived in pleasure." It is a translation of the Greek word *truphao*, which depicts *a luxurious life* or *one who lives self-indulgently*. Similarly, James said these unjust employers were "wanton," which in Greek is the word *spatalao*, and it means *to live extravagantly*, *to indulge in luxury*, *to live wastefully*, or *to live with no indulgent restriction*. Essentially, it is the picture of *lewd living*.

Hence, these corrupt landowners were living unrestrained lives of decadence. Furthermore, the Bible says they had "nourished their hearts." The Greek word for "nourished" here is *trepho*, and it means *nourished*; *fed*; *fattened*; or *enlarged*. The phrase "your hearts" in Greek is *tas kardias humon*, which literally means *the hearts of you*. The inclusion of the word *humon* once again tells us James' words don't refer to every employer, but only to this particular category of individuals who have unjustly treated their workers.

God Is Giving Them Time To Repent

When we come to verse 6, James caps off his examination of the ruthless rich by offering this stinging indictment:

> Ye have condemned and killed the just; and he doth not resist you.
> —James 5:6

In this verse, the word "killed" is a form of the Greek term *phoneuo*, meaning *to kill, to murder, to commit homicide, to intentionally murder*, or *to slaughter*. Although it certainly signifies physical murder, it can also refer to not treating people correctly. James said these ruthless employers had killed "the just"— which in Greek is *ton dikaion*. Here again we see a definite article with the word *dikaios*, which means it would be better translated *THE just; THE upright; THE ones who have done right and are right in the sight of God*.

To the best of their ability, these honorable workers had given their all, and yet their corrupt employers had not paid them adequately. Ironically, James said, "…And he [God] doth not resist you" (James 5:6). The word "not" is the Greek word *ouk*, which is *an emphatic not* and communicates *not* in the strongest of terms. The word "resist" is *antitassomai*, and it means *to stand against* or *to set one's self against something or someone else*.

Basically, James is informing us that in spite of these rich men who could certainly treat their workers better but are not, God has not set Himself against them. Instead, He is giving them time to repent and make things right. He wants everyone to repent and live justly, but here James addresses employers.

Nevertheless, God says, "If you have the ability to do good to your workers and you're not doing it, you're wrong. And I — the Lord of Sabaoth — will come with My armies to set things in order." This is a very serious and sobering statement God is making to anyone who is an employer of others.

Friend, if you're employed and you feel that you're not being paid correctly, remember that your cries for justice are reaching the ears of the Lord. He is not ignorant of what you're going through, and He is going to move on your behalf.

STUDY QUESTIONS

Study to shew thyself approved unto God, a workman that needeth not to be ashamed, rightly dividing the word of truth.
— 2 Timothy 2:15

1. In God's eyes, the most important and cherished thing on earth is people, which is why He has so much to say in His Word about how we treat one another. Jesus made a statement over 2,000 years ago, which is just as valid today as it was then. Look up and write out this "golden rule" for living recorded in Mark 7:12 and Luke 6:31. What other verses does this remind you of?

2. We saw in this lesson that nothing is hidden from God's sight (*see* Hebrews 4:13) and that He hears the cries of those in trouble. How do Psalm 34:9-20 and 145:14-21 expand your understanding of who God hears and helps?

3. According to Isaiah 59:1,2, what can often hinder our prayers from being answered? What remedy does David reveal in Psalm 32:1-7 for breaking free from this hindrance?

PRACTICAL APPLICATION

> But be ye doers of the word, and not hearers only,
> deceiving your own selves.
> —James 1:22

1. God's Word says the money that wealthy employers had stockpiled would be summoned to testify *against* their unscrupulous actions. Although you may not be a business owner who has employees, there are times when you pay someone for providing you with a service — such as a waitress in a restaurant. If your money were called upon by God to give testimony about you, what do you think it would say about *your* actions?

2. James tells us that when a person hires someone to do a job and they fail to pay the worker a fair wage, it releases a septic-like infection in their lives. Have you ever treated a worker unfairly or underpaid them for a job they did for you? If so, what were the side-effects? Did you ever ask God to forgive you and make things right with the person?

3. In the First Century, certain well-off landowners were cheating their hired hands, holding back from them what was rightfully theirs. How about you? Have you ever had an employer underpay you or rob you of credit for a job you did? How did you respond? What new insights is this teaching from James 5 giving you?

LESSON 2

TOPIC

The Lord Is Coming Soon

SCRIPTURES

1. **James 5:7-11** — Be patient therefore, brethren, unto the coming of the Lord. Behold, the husbandman waiteth for the precious fruit of the earth, and hath long patience for it, until he receive the early and latter rain. Be ye also patient; stablish your hearts: for the coming of the Lord draweth nigh. Grudge not one against another, brethren, lest ye be condemned: behold, the judge standeth before the door. Take, my brethren, the prophets, who have spoken in the name of the Lord,

for an example of suffering affliction, and of patience. Behold, we count them happy which endure. Ye have heard of the patience of Job, and have seen the end of the Lord; that the Lord is very pitiful, and of tender mercy.

GREEK WORDS

1. "patient" — μακροθυμέω (*makrothumeo*): the patient restraint of anger and therefore denotes longsuffering; can be translated as the words forbearance and patience; its action is like unto a candle with a very long wick, it can burn a long time; it is ready to forbear, to wait patiently, to be longsuffering, as it patiently waits for an event or for a result to transpire; it can refer to the patient restraint of anger, long-suffering, forbearance, or patience
2. "therefore" — οὖν (*oun*): a conjunction; as a result; consequently
3. "brethren" — ἀδελφός (*adelphos*): a term used to describe two or more who were born from the same womb; an endearing term used to describe those of one's own family; later used in a military sense to depict brothers in battle; a comrade; hence, brotherhood
4. "unto" — ἕως (*heos*): till; as far as; up to; until
5. "coming" — παρουσία (*parousia*): a technical expression for the royal visit of a king, or emperor; the arrival of one who alone can deal with a situation; used here to denote the coming of Christ for the Church
6. "Lord" — κύριος (*kurios*): lord, or supreme master
7. "behold" — ἰδού (*idou*): bewilderment, shock, amazement, and wonder
8. "husbandman" — γεωργός (*georgos*): a farmer who tills the soil, plants the seed, pulls the weeds, and reaps the harvest
9. "waiteth" — ἐκδέχομαι (*echdechomai*): from ἐκ (*ek*) and δέχομαι (*dechomai*); ἐκ (*ek*) means out, and δέχομαι (*dechomai*) means to welcome or to gladly receive; compounded, to wait, to anticipate; a wide-open arms reception
10. "long patience" — μακροθυμέω (*makrothumeo*): the patient restraint of anger and therefore denotes longsuffering; can be translated as words forbearance and patience; its action is like unto a candle with a very long wick, it can burn a long time; it is ready to forbear, to wait patiently, to be longsuffering, as it patiently waits for an event or for a result to transpire; it can refer to the patient restraint of anger, long-suffering, forbearance, or patience

11. "until" — ἕως (*heos*): till; as far as; up to; until
12. "receive" — λαμβάνω (*lambano*): to lay hold of something in order to make it your very own, almost like a person who reaches out to grab, to capture, or to take possession of something; in some cases, it means to violently lay hold of something in order to seize and take it as one's very own; at other times it depicts one who graciously receives something that is freely and easily given
13. "early" — πρώϊμος (*proimos*): the early rain, which fell from October
14. "latter" — ὄψιμος (*opsimos*): the latter rain, which falls chiefly in the months of March and April just before the harvest
15. "stablish" — στηρίζω (*steridzo*): fixed and solid, like a column that holds up the roof of a house; to brace, to shore up, to bolster, to support, or to uphold; it fundamentally describes the act of adding strength and support to something already existing; used to describe a rod driven into the ground next to a grapevine to support the grapevine as it grew upward; the supporting stake supported the clusters of grapes that eventually hung on the vine
16. "Lord" — κύριος (*kurios*): lord, or supreme master
17. "draweth nigh" — ἐγγίζω (*engidzo*): to closely approach; extremely close
18. "grudge not" — μὴ στενάζετε (*me stenadzete*): μὴ with στενάζω (*stenadzo*), to moan, groan, or sigh; an expression of deeply felt emotion; to vent or to aspirate; in this verse, do not negatively moan, groan, or sigh
19. "against" — κατ' (*kat'*): literally against, as upset with, or in opposition to
20. "another" — ἀλλήλων (*allelon*): each other; reciprocally; of each other
21. "judge" — κριτής (*krites*): pictures Christ as a judge, magistrate, or ruler; one who passes judgment; where we get the word critic
22. "standeth" — ἵστημι (*histemi*): stand; to be set
23. "before" — πρό (*pro*): a preposition meaning before, right in front of
24. "door" — θύρα (*thura*): a large and solid door; such doors were usually locked with a heavy bolt that slid through rings attached to the door and the frame; when such doors were opened, it provided access that was normally restricted, and hence, it could denote an opportunity
25. "take… as an example" — ὑπόδειγμα (*hupodeigma*): used to picture a student who is learning to copy the letters of the alphabet

26. "suffering affliction" — **κακοπάθεια** (*kakopatheia*): from **κακός** (*ka-kos*) which describes something foul, and the word **πάθος** (*pathos*): which describes suffering usually of an emotional or mental type; putting up with emotional or mental hardness; emotional or mental toughness

SYNOPSIS

We have noted that James was writing to a group of First-Century believers who were exasperated with what they were experiencing in life. Due to intense persecution, they had been scattered all over the eastern lands of the Roman Empire, and as a result, they had lost their homes, their businesses, and their income. Even worse, many of them had been separated from their family members and were not able to find them.

It seems that before this scattering took place, these believers were very prosperous — many of them even owned their own businesses. But now they were employees of others, and in some cases serving like slaves, with very little compensation for the work they were performing. Needless to say, they were quite upset and began to cry out to God to avenge them for the mistreatment they endured.

For this reason, James wrote them and informed them in Chapter 5 that when people are paid unjustly and they call out to God, He hears their cry for help and steps in to bring justice to the oppressed.

The emphasis of this lesson:

James instructs us to be patient with one another right up till the coming of the Lord. Just as a farmer patiently waits for the seed to take root and produce a harvest, we're to wait for godly fruit to be produced in our life and the lives of others. When we become impatient, we have to focus our attention on strengthening our heart and remind ourselves that Jesus' return is imminent. He will make all things right when He comes.

God's Word tells us in Deuteronomy 32:35 that vengeance belongs to the Lord alone. With this knowledge, James urged his readers not to take matters into their own hands. Instead, he encouraged them to…

> **Be patient therefore, brethren, unto the coming of the Lord. Behold, the husbandman waiteth for the precious fruit of the**

earth, and hath long patience for it, until he receive the early and latter rain.

Be ye also patient; stablish your hearts: for the coming of the Lord draweth nigh.

Grudge not one against another, brethren, lest ye be condemned: behold, the judge standeth before the door.

Take, my brethren, the prophets, who have spoken in the name of the Lord, for an example of suffering affliction, and of patience.

Behold, we count them happy which endure. Ye have heard of the patience of Job, and have seen the end of the Lord; that the Lord is very pitiful, and of tender mercy.
—James 5:7-11

Let's unpack the rich meaning of these five verses to see more clearly what James was saying to these First-Century believers and to us.

We Are To Be 'Patient' Right Up to the Coming of the Lord

After letting us know about God's awareness and disapproval of corrupt employers and landowners, James said, "Be patient therefore, brethren, unto the coming of the Lord. Behold, the husbandman waiteth for the precious fruit of the earth, and hath long patience for it, until he receive the early and latter rain" (James 5:7).

The word "patient" here is the Greek word *makrothumeo*. It is a compound of the word *makros*, which describes something *very long*, and the word *thumos*, which describes *a strong, growing passion*. When these words are joined to form *makrothumeo*, it signifies *the patient restraint of anger* and therefore denotes *longsuffering*. It can be translated as the words *forbearance* and *patience*. Its action is like unto a candle with a very long wick that can burn a long time. Thus, a person who is "patient" (*makrothumeo*) is ready to *forbear*, to *wait patiently*, and to *be longsuffering*, as he patiently waits for an event or for a result to transpire.

Essentially, James is telling his listeners, "Burn long like a candle with a very long wick. Wait for people to 'come around,' listen to counsel, make progress, and ultimately implement change in their lives."

Again, notice James addressed his readers as "brethren"— the Greek word *adelphos* — a term used to describe *two or more who were born from the same womb*. This endearing term was not only used multiple times by James, but also by Peter, John, and Paul in their writings. It describes *those of one's own family*; hence, all God's children who are related in Christ and born from the spiritual womb of God.

James said, "Be patient therefore brethren..." (James 5:7). The word "therefore" in Greek is the word *oun*, which is a conjunction and means *accordingly*, *consequently*, or *as a result*. James urged his audience — which includes *us* — to be longsuffering with our brothers and sisters in Christ "...unto the coming of the Lord..." (James 5:7).

The word "unto" is *heos* in the Greek, and it means *as far as*, *until*, or *right up to*. In this case, it indicates *right up to the coming of the Lord*. In Greek, the word "coming" is *parousia*, which is a technical expression for *the royal visit of a king, or emperor*. It is *the arrival of one who alone can deal with a situation*, and here it's used to denote the coming of Christ for the Church.

Basically, James is saying, "My brothers, although things seem to be unjust and difficult, when the Lord Jesus comes (*parousia*), He will come with the authority and power to set everything straight." The word "Lord" here is the Greek word *kurios*, which means *lord* or *supreme master*. In spite of the injustice we may be experiencing, one day soon the Supreme Master and Lord, Jesus Christ is going to arrive on the scene and make things right.

It Takes the Fullness of God's Work To Produce Full Maturity in Our Lives

To help us better understand the meaning of patience, James gives us this: "...Behold, the husbandman waiteth for the precious fruit of the earth, and hath long patience for it, until he receive the early and latter rain" (James 5:7).

The word "behold" here is *idou*, and it describes *bewilderment, shock, amazement, and wonder*. The use of this word is the equivalent of James saying, "Wow! What I'm about to say is absolutely amazing...." Then he talks about the "husbandman," which is the Greek word *georgos* and describes *a farmer who tills the soil, plants the seed, pulls the weeds, and reaps the harvest*.

As you may know, farming is a long, drawn-out process, which is why James said the husbandman "waiteth." This word is a translation of the Greek word *echdechomai*, from the words *ek* and *dechomai*. The word *ek* means *out*, and *dechomai* means *to welcome* or *to gladly receive*. When these words are compounded, the new word *echdechomai* means *to wait* or *to anticipate* with *a wide-open arms reception*.

Just as farmers wait with great anticipation and patience for the precious fruit of the earth to burst forth from all the seed they've planted and cared for, we too are to wait with long patience and great anticipation for what God has promised. The Greek word for "long patience" here is again *makrothumeo*, which is *the patient restraint of anger* and therefore denotes *longsuffering, forbearance*, and *patience*. Instead of becoming frustrated and frazzled by what we're experiencing, God is telling us through James that we are to burn a long time like a candle with a very long wick. We are to be ready to forbear, to wait patiently, and to be longsuffering, as we patiently wait for an event or for a result to transpire.

James said that a farmer waits patiently and expectantly "…until he receive the early and latter rain" (James 5:7). The word "until" is again the Greek word *heos*, meaning *till; as far as; up to;* or *until*. Farmers waited *right up to the point* of receiving both the early and latter rain for their crops.

There were two seasons of rain that came to Israel: the *early rain*, which took place in late September and October, and the *latter rain*, which occurred primarily in March and April just before the harvest. Although the early rain was always exciting because it caused the crops to start growing, the plants could not reach maturity until they received the latter rain. In the same way, we cannot expect to reap a harvest after only the initial outpouring or move of God in our lives. We must wait patiently for the full cycle of His outpouring in our lives — including the latter rain.

This brings us to the word "receive," which is a form of the Greek word *lambano*, meaning *to lay hold of something in order to make it your very own*. It is the picture of *a person who reaches out to grab, to capture*, or *to take possession of something*. In some cases, it means *to violently lay hold of something in order to seize and take it as one's very own*. At other times it depicts *one who graciously receives something that is freely and easily given*. God gives us what we desire, but we have to wait for the right moment to seize it and make it our own.

Strengthening Our Heart
Helps Us Be Patient

James goes on to say, "Be ye also patient; stablish your hearts: for the coming of the Lord draweth nigh" (James 5:8). Here, for the third time in two verses, we see the Greek word *makrothumeo* — translated as "patient." It is the compound of the word *makros*, which describes something *very long*, and the word *thumos*, which denotes *a strong, growing passion*. When compounded, the word *makrothumeo* describes *the patient restraint of anger* and therefore denotes *longsuffering*. It can also be translated as words *forbearance* and *patience*, and its action can be compared to a candle with a very long wick that can burn a long time.

Hence, James is counseling his readers to be ready to forbear, to wait patiently, and to be longsuffering, as they patiently wait for the desired results to transpire. Likewise, he says to "stablish your hearts." This word "stablish" — the Greek word *steridzo* — means *to be fixed and solid*, like a column that holds up the roof of a house. Moreover, it means *to brace, to shore up, to bolster, to support,* or *to uphold*. This word *steridzo* fundamentally describes *the act of adding strength and support to something already existing*. This very word was used to describe a rod driven into the ground next to a grapevine to support the grapevine as it grew upward; the supporting stake reinforced the clusters of grapes that eventually hung on the vine.

Why does James urge us to be patient and "stablish" (*steridzo*) our hearts? Because when we're impatient, we're most likely staring at our circumstances, becoming frustrated and irritated by what we see happening. Essentially, James is saying, "Get your eyes off of your circumstances and focus on your heart." If we'll bolster, support, and add strength to our heart, we can deal with anything that comes our way.

The reason for adjusting our focus is because "…the coming of the Lord draweth nigh" (James 5:8). Once more we see the word "coming," which is the Greek word *parousia*, a technical expression for *the royal visit of a king or emperor*. Specifically, it depicts *the arrival of one who alone can deal with a situation and put things in order*. Here it is used to denote the coming of the Lord Jesus Christ for the Church.

Again, the word "Lord" is the Greek term *kurios*, meaning *lord* or *supreme master*. When Jesus — the Supreme Master and Lord over all — returns to the earth, He will most certainly make all things right, and according to James, Jesus' coming "draweth nigh." This phrase is a translation of the Greek word *engidzo*, which means *to closely approach* or be *extremely close*.

Don't Blow Your Top or Moan and Groan About Others

Knowing that the Lord's coming is extremely close, James further instructed his readers, "Grudge not one against another, brethren, lest ye be condemned: behold, the judge standeth before the door" (James 5:9).

We've noted in our previous studies on the book of James that there was a great deal of fighting and bickering going on among these believers. Some were very upset as they watched others have their prayers answered and be blessed abundantly while they were still waiting for God to step in and bless them. Consequently, believers began judging and grudging one another. That's why James said, "Grudge not one against another, brethren…" (James 5:9).

In Greek, the words "grudge not" are a compound of the words *me* and *stenadzo*. The word *me* is a strong negative, and the word *stenadzo* means *to moan, groan,* or *sigh*. It is *an expression of deeply felt emotion* and carries the idea of *venting, aspirating,* or *blowing one's top*. In this verse, "grudge not" (*me stenadzete*) means *do not negatively moan, groan, or sigh* against one another.

The word "against" is a form of the Greek word *kat'*, which literally means *against* and depicts *one person being upset with or in opposition to another*. Rather than rejoice with those who were experiencing blessings and breakthroughs, they were at odds with one another.

In Greek, this word "another" is the word *allelon*, and it describes *reciprocating action* toward each other. In other words, what one was giving out, they were also getting back in return. It is the law of sowing and reaping. Therefore, when James said, "Grudge not one against another," he was urging his audience not to be involved in the reciprocal bad behavior of exploding and venting anger against each other. Why? Because they were "brethren" — *adelphos* — which means brothers in Christ, born from the womb of God, fighting as *comrades* against the same enemy.

Jesus Is at the Door Just About To Return

Then James makes this powerful statement: "…Behold, the judge standeth before the door" (James 5:9). This is the third reference in three verses that points to Christ's return. Again, we see the word "behold," which is the Greek word *idou*, describing *bewilderment, shock, amazement,* and *wonder*. James is in awe of the fact that the "judge standeth before the door."

In Greek, the word "judge" is *krites*, which is from where we get the word *critic*. It pictures *Christ as a judge, magistrate, or ruler*. It is *one who passes judgment* or *the judge who is going to bring everything back into order*. James says, "…[He] standeth before the door" (James 5:9).

The word "standeth" in Greek is *histemi*, which means *to stand* or *to be set*. The word "before" — the Greek word *pro* — is a preposition meaning *before* or *right in front of*. And the word "door" is the Greek term *thura*, which describes *a large and solid door*. Such doors were usually locked with a heavy bolt that slid through rings attached to the door and the frame. When such doors were opened, it gave access that was normally restricted. Hence, this word *thura* could denote *an opportunity*.

Jesus is standing right in front of the spiritual door that separates Heaven and earth. Although it is a heavy, solid door that has been closed, Jesus is about ready to open it and return to earth to come and get us and bring us into eternity with Him.

By Studying the Lives of the Prophets We Can Develop Mental and Emotional Endurance

When we come to verse 10, James says, "Take, my brethren, the prophets, who have spoken in the name of the Lord, for an example of suffering affliction, and of patience" (James 5:10). In the original Greek, the verse actually opens by saying, "Take as an example," which is a translation of the Greek word *hupodeigma*. This word was used to picture *a student who is learning to copy the letters of the alphabet*. James specifically chose this word to encourage his readers to become like a student and study those who have lived before them. Particularly, he referred to the prophets who spoke in the Name of the Lord and who suffered affliction patiently.

The words "suffering affliction" is the Greek word *kakopatheia*, which is a compound of the word *ka-kos* and *pathos*. The word *ka-kos* describes something *foul*, and the word *pathos* describes *suffering* usually of *an emotional or mental type*. When these words are compounded to form *kakopatheia*, it means *to put up with something foul by means of emotional or mental hardness*. It is the development of *emotional* or *mental toughness*.

James goes on to say, "Behold, we count them happy which endure…" (James 5:11). *The phrase "count them happy"* in Greek means *ridiculously happy*. Indeed, those who endure are blessed with all kinds of blessings and benefits.

The word "endure" is the Greek word *hupomeno*, which means *to abide* or *to stay in one's spot*, *to keep your position* or *to resolve to maintain territory that you've gained*. In a military sense, it pictures soldiers ordered to maintain their positions even in the face of opposition. Moreover, this word *hupomeno* means *to defiantly stick it out regardless of pressures mounted against it*. It is *staying power* or *hang-in-there power*. It is *the attitude that holds out, holds on, outlast, perseveres, hangs in there, never giving up and refusing to surrender to obstacles and turning down every opportunity to quit*.

We are urged by James, the half-brother of Jesus, to take as an example the prophets of the Old Testament who developed mental and emotional toughness to endure great hardships for the glory of the Lord. Like a child learning his ABCs, we are to closely study how they lived and copy it in our own lives.

In our next lesson, we will learn what James meant when he said, "…Let your yea be yea; and your nay, nay; lest ye fall into condemnation" (James 5:12).

STUDY QUESTIONS

Study to shew thyself approved unto God, a workman that needeth not to be ashamed, rightly dividing the word of truth.
— 2 Timothy 2:15

1. Have you become impatient with others or yourself? If so, where is your focus? Are you staring at your circumstances or the failures of people? What does Hebrews 12:2,3 say you are to do to help you break free from this frustration? (Also consider Philippians 2:5-11.)
2. To rise above the irritation of impatience, James said, "Focus on strengthening your heart." What are some practical steps you can take

to bolster, support, and add strength to your heart? As you answer, consider Proverbs 4:20-23; Joshua 1:8; Deuteronomy 6:6; 11:18; and Colossians 3:16.

PRACTICAL APPLICATION

> But be ye doers of the word, and not hearers only, deceiving your own selves.
> —James 1:22

1. Just as a candle with a long wick burns a long time, God wants us to be patient with fellow believers as they grow and mature into the character of Christ. Who can you think of that patiently put up with your immaturity? What type of childish behaviors has the Holy Spirit helped you grow out of?
2. When James wrote his letter, he repeatedly told his readers, "...The coming of the Lord draweth nigh" (James 5:8). Knowing that he wrote this nearly 2,000 years ago, what does this tell you about the nearness of the Lord's return? How does this help you trust Jesus to make all things right when He comes?
3. The Bible tells us, "Grudge not one against another, brethren..." (James 5:9), which means don't *moan* and *groan* against other believers. Be honest. Are you grumbling and complaining like this? If so, who is it about? What are they doing that bothers you so greatly? How might God be using this person's shortcomings to bring maturity in your life? (Consider Matthew 7:3-6; Romans 2:1.)

LESSON 3

TOPIC

Let Your 'Yea Be Yea' and Your 'Nay Be Nay'

SCRIPTURES

1. **James 5:10-12** — Take, my brethren, the prophets, who have spoken in the name of the Lord, for an example of suffering affliction, and

of patience. Behold, we count them happy which endure. Ye have heard of the patience of Job, and have seen the end of the Lord; that the Lord is very pitiful, and of tender mercy. But above all things, my brethren, swear not, neither by heaven, neither by the earth, neither by any other oath: but let your yea be yea; and your nay, nay; lest ye fall into condemnation.

2. **Matthew 5:34-37** — But I say unto you, Swear not at all; neither by heaven; for it is God's throne: nor by the earth; for it is his footstool: neither by Jerusalem; for it is the city of the great King. Neither shalt thou swear by thy head, because thou canst not make one hair white or black. But let your communication be, Yea, yea; Nay, nay: for whatsoever is more than these cometh of evil.

GREEK WORDS

1. "take… as an example" — ὑπόδειγμα (*hupodeigma*): used to picture a student who is learning to copy the letters of the alphabet
2. "brethren" — ἀδελφός (*adelphos*): a term used to describe two or more who were born from the same womb; an endearing term used to describe those of one's own family; later used in a military sense to depict brothers in battle; a comrade; hence, brotherhood
3. "suffering affliction" — κακοπάθεια (*kakopatheia*): from κακός (*ka-kos*) which describes something foul, and the word πάθος (*pathos*) which describes suffering usually of an emotional or mental type; putting up with emotional or mental hardness; emotional or mental toughness
4. "behold" — ἰδού (*idou*): bewilderment, shock, amazement, and wonder
5. "count them happy" — μακαρίζω (*makaridzo*): to count supremely blessed; happy and blessed with all kinds of benefits
6. "endure" — ὑπομένω (*hupomeno*): to stay or abide; to remain in one's spot; to keep a position; to resolve to maintain territory gained; in a military sense, it pictures soldiers ordered to maintain their positions even in the face of opposition; to defiantly stick it out regardless of pressures mounted against it; staying power; hang-in-there power; the attitude that holds out, holds on, outlasts, perseveres, and hangs in there, never giving up, refusing to surrender to obstacles, and turning down every opportunity to quit; it pictures one who is under a heavy load but refuses to bend, break, or surrender because he is convinced

that the territory, promise, or principle under assault rightfully belongs to him

7. "patience" — ὑπομονή (*hupomone*): to stay or abide; to remain in one's spot; to keep a position; to resolve to maintain territory gained; in a military sense, it pictures soldiers ordered to maintain their positions even in the face of opposition; to defiantly stick it out regardless of pressures mounted against it; staying power; hang-in-there power; the attitude that holds out, holds on, outlasts, perseveres, and hangs in there, never giving up, refusing to surrender to obstacles, and turning down every opportunity to quit; it pictures one who is under a heavy load but refuses to bend, break, or surrender because he is convinced that the territory, promise, or principle under assault rightfully belongs to him

8. "seen" — ὁράω (*horao*): to see; to behold; to perceive; to know from observation

9. "end" — τέλος (*telos*): the conclusion; the outcome; the end

10. "that" — ὅτι (*hoti*): explicitly that

11. "very pitiful" — πολύσπλαγχνος (*polusplagchagnos*): a compound of πολύς (*polus*) and σπλάγχνα (*splagchna*); the word πολύς (*polus*) means great in number or plenteous; σπλάγχνα (*splagchna*) means bowels; compounded, "many-boweled" and full of affection

12. "tender mercy" — οἰκτιρμός (*oiktirmos*): a deep compassion, feeling, or pity about someone else's condition or situation

13. "but" — δέ (*de*): an exclamatory marker; categorically; emphatically

14. "above all" — Πρὸ πάντων (*pro panton*): above all else

15. "swear" — ὀμνύω (*omnuo*): to swear; to make an oath; pictures a rash or threatening oath; one who is swearing that he will take matters into his own hands

16. "neither" — μήτε (*mete*): neither; never ever; keep it out of the realm of possibility; don't go there

17. "by heaven" — οὐρανός (*ouranos*): heaven

18. "by the earth" — γῆ (*ge*): the earth

19. "by any other oath" — ἄλλον τινὰ ὅρκον (*allon tina horkon*): by any other pledge, oath, or threat

20. "yea be yea" — τὸ Ναὶ, ναί (*nai, nai*): the Yes mean yes

21. "nay, nay" — τὸ Οὖ, οὖ (*Ou, ou*): the No means no

22. "ye fall" — πίπτω (*pipto*): to fall; a downward plummet; to fall into a terrible predicament or into a worse state than he was in before; someone who falls into some type of failure
23. "into" — ὑπὸ (*hupo*): better translated, under
24. "condemnation" — κρίσις (*krisis*): judgment; judgment by others or self-inflicted judgment; where we get the word crisis; hence, fall into a crisis situation; possibly pictures one who makes matters worse and creates a worse crisis; hence, self-inflicted troubles

SYNOPSIS

We have seen that the believers James was writing to were former Jews from the 12 tribes of Israel, which had been scattered abroad all across the eastern lands of the Mediterranean (*see* James 1:1). The words "scattered abroad" in this verse are a translation of the Greek word *diaspora*, a very specific word that describes *the random scattering of seed*. When a farmer planted seed in his field, he could methodically plant one seed after another in a nice, neat row. Or he could reach his hand into a satchel, grab a handful of seed, and begin throwing it randomly all over the field. That is exactly what the word *diaspora* depicts.

In this case, it was the random scattering of believers as a result of Roman persecution during the First Century. They had lost their homes, their jobs, their finances, their businesses, and many had even lost connection with their family members. Deeply discouraged, they began to wonder, *Is God allowing all these disastrous events to take place? Is all of this suffering somehow His will for our lives?*

In their distress, these believers from all across the Roman Empire began writing to James, expressing their deep frustrations and struggles. Feeling as though their lives were crushed, they asked him to explain what was going on. Prior to the scattering, many had been very prosperous — several had even owned their own business. But once the dispersion took place, they had to go to work for others at very low-paying jobs.

After waiting and praying for things to improve but seeing no change, a number of believers were considering taking matters into their own hands to try and regain what they felt was rightfully theirs. This was James' primary reason for writing his fifth chapter.

The emphasis of this lesson:

The prophets serve as an example of how to handle affliction. Those who endure hardship, pressing all the way through to the end, become a possessor of everything that belongs to us in Christ. The Lord is deeply moved by the hardships we face and has promised to bring about justice in our lives. Therefore, we must resist the temptation to make rash vows and take matters into our own hands.

The Prophets Serve As an Example of How To Handle Affliction

In order to help these beaten-down believers regain hope, James wrote to them and said, "Take, my brethren, the prophets, who have spoken in the name of the Lord, for an example of suffering affliction, and of patience" (James 5:10). What's interesting is that in the original Greek, the text actually opens with the words, "Take as an example." This phrase is a translation of the Greek word *hupodeigma*, a word used to picture *a student who is learning to copy by hand the letters of the alphabet*.

By using this word, James was telling his readers to become like students — to study the prophets who had lived before them and learn what they did when they went through tough times. As they examined the prophets and learned what they did and didn't do, they were to copy their behavior.

Notice how James addressed his readers. Once more, he called them "brethren," using the Greek word *adelphos*, a term used to describe *two or more who were born from the same womb*. This same endearing term was later made famous by the legendary warrior Alexander the Great. In a military sense, it became known to depict *brothers in battle*; *a comrade*; or *a brotherhood*. By calling his readers "brethren" (*adelphos*), James was placing himself on their level down in the trenches, telling them as one brother to another who they should be studying and emulating in their lives.

Particularly, James pointed to the prophets "…who [had] spoken in the name of the Lord, for an example of suffering affliction, and of patience" (James 5:10). The words "suffering affliction" in Greek is *kakopatheia*, which is a compound of the word *ka-kos* and *pathos*. The word *ka-kos* denotes something *foul*, and the word *pathos* usually describes *suffering connected with the emotions or mind*. When these words are compounded to form *kakopatheia*, it means *to mentally and emotionally put up with something foul*; it is the picture of *mental* or *emotional toughness*.

James went on to say, "Behold, we count them happy which endure…" (James 5:11). Here again, we see the word "behold," which is the Greek word *idou*, describing *bewilderment, shock, amazement*, and *wonder*. It is as though James is looking at his readers and saying, "Wow! Look at what happens to those who endure…."

Then he adds, "…We count them happy…" (James 5:11). This phrase is a translation of the Greek word *makaridzo*, which means *to count supremely blessed* or *to be happy and blessed with all kinds of benefits*. Those who endure hardship, pressing all the way through to the end, become a possessor of everything that belongs to us in Christ.

What Does It Mean To 'Endure'? How Is It Related to the Word 'Patience'?

The word "endure" is the Greek word *hupomeno*, which means *to stay or abide* or *to remain in one's spot*. One who endures is *one who keeps his position* or *resolves to maintain territory he's gained*. In a military sense, it pictures soldiers ordered to maintain their positions even in the face of opposition. Moreover, the word *hupomeno* — translated here as "endure"— means *to defiantly stick it out regardless of pressures mounted against it*.

One expositor calls it *staying power*, and another says it's *hang-in-there power*. It is *the attitude that holds out, holds on, outlasts, perseveres, and hangs in there, never giving up and refusing to surrender to obstacles, and turning down every opportunity to quit*. It pictures one who is under a heavy load but refuses to bend, break, or surrender because he is convinced that the territory, promise, or principle under assault rightfully belongs to him.

James said to take as an example the prophets of the Old Testament. They developed mental and emotional toughness and endured great hardships for the glory of the Lord. Then he points to a specific person, saying, "…Ye have heard of the patience of Job, and have seen the end of the Lord; that the Lord is very pitiful, and of tender mercy" (James 5:11).

Notice James singles out Job as having noteworthy *patience*. Unfortunately, many religious people today think of him as a victim of circumstance — a man who lost his family, his fortune, and everything dear to him. But a closer look at this verse in James' letter gives us a new insight into the story of Job. It says, "...Ye have heard of the patience of Job..." (James 5:11). Can you guess what the Greek word for "patience" is here? If you said *hupomone*, you are right.

Isn't it interesting that the Holy Spirit prompted James to use the same Greek word twice in one verse? And this second occurrence specifically describes Job. This tells us a great deal about his character. It means Job made an internal decision *to stay, abide, and remain in his place*. He kept his position and resolved to maintain the territory he had gained. Like a soldier ordered to maintain his position even in the face of opposition, Job chose to defiantly stick it out regardless of pressures mounted against him. Through all he experienced, he maintained the attitude that holds out, holds on, outlasts, perseveres, and hangs in there, never giving up, refusing to surrender to obstacles, and turning down every opportunity to quit. That is what the word *hupomone* — translated here as "patience" — means, and that is the word James chose to describe Job.

The Lord Is Deeply Moved by the Hardships We Experience

James continues by saying, "...[You] have seen the end of the Lord; that the Lord is very pitiful, and of tender mercy" (James 5:11). The word "seen" is the Greek word *horao*, which means *to see; to behold; to perceive;* or *to know from observation*. The way we "see" the story of Job is by reading the book that bears his name — one that is understood to be the oldest book of the Bible.

When the Bible says we have "seen the end," the word "end" is the Greek word *telos*, which describes *the conclusion, the outcome,* or *the end*. The conclusion of Job's life was phenomenal, which is why James said, "...that the Lord is very pitiful, and of tender mercy" (James 5:11). The word "that" in Greek is *hoti*, which is *a pointer word* explicitly pointing to something very important. In this case, it's pointing to the marvelous conclusion of Job's life and how the Lord was "...very pitiful, and of tender mercy" (James 5:11).

The phrase "very pitiful" is a translation of the unique Greek word *polusplagchagnos*, which is a compound of the words *polus* and *splagchna*. The word *polus* means *great in number* or *plenteous*; and *splagchna* is literally the Greek word for *bowels*. When compounded, the new word *polusplagchagnos* — translated here as "very pitiful" — literally means *many-boweled* but would be better translated as *full of affection*. It indicates that the Lord was — and *is* — deeply moved by what we go through in life. As a result, He is filled with "tender mercy."

The Greek word for "tender mercy" here is *oiktirmos*, and it describes *a deep compassion, feeling,* or *pity about someone else's condition or situation*. This tells us that when God sees His children in trouble, He's moved with compassion to step in and act on our behalf. This is a powerful promise we need to remember — especially when we go through trying times.

Regardless of What's Happening, Don't Take Matters Into Your Own Hands

After instructing us to study the prophets and consider the example of Job and how the Lord mercifully moved on his behalf to restore what the enemy had stolen, James said, "But above all things, my brethren, swear not, neither by heaven, neither by the earth, neither by any other oath: but let your yea be yea; and your nay, nay; lest ye fall into condemnation" (James 5:12).

There is much to learn from this verse, starting with the opening word "but." In Greek, it's the word *de*, which is an exclamatory marker, meaning *categorically* or *emphatically*. Then he said, "above all" — which in Greek is *pro panton* and means *above all else*. James then addressed his readers once more as "brethren," which is the Greek word *adelphos*, a term used to describe *two or more who were born from the same womb*. The reason he used this endearing term again and again was to promote and preserve the common bond of comradery and brotherhood he had with his readers.

"Swear not," James warned, "neither by heaven, neither by the earth, neither by any other oath…" (James 5:12). The word "swear" here is the Greek word *omnuo*, which means *to swear* or *to make an oath*. It pictures *a rash or threatening oath; one who is swearing that he will take matters into his own hands*. Keep in mind, James was addressing a number of people who were tired of the injustice they were experiencing and worn out from waiting for things to turn around for the better. The temptation to take matters into their own hands was at an all-time high, which is why James said, "Above everything else, I emphatically appeal to you, don't do this…."

Let Your *Yes* Mean *Yes* and Your *No* Mean *No*

Specifically, James said not to swear "…neither by heaven, neither by the earth, neither by any other oath…" (James 5:12). The word "neither," which appears three times in this verse, is the Greek word *mete*, and it means *neither* or *never ever*. It indicates *keeping something out of the realm of possibility* and is the equivalent of saying, "Don't go there."

Therefore, we are not to swear or speak a threatening oath "by heaven" or "by the earth." In Greek, the phrase "by heaven" is the word *ouranos*, the word for *heaven*; and the phrase "by the earth" is derived from the Greek word *ge*, which is the word for *the earth*. When James says swear not "by any other oath," it means *by any other pledge, oath, or threat*.

These instructions are very similar to the command Jesus gave in Matthew 5:34-37 where He said, "…Swear not at all; neither by heaven; for it is God's throne: nor by the earth; for it is his footstool: neither by Jerusalem; for it is the city of the great King. Neither shalt thou swear by thy head, because thou canst not make one hair white or black. But let your communication be, Yea, yea; Nay, nay: for whatsoever is more than these cometh of evil."

Any time a person begins to swear, they have crossed a line and are headed for trouble. That's what Jesus is saying here and what James reiterates in verse 12. Rather than make rash, threatening oaths that tend toward evil, he said, "…But let your yea be yea; and your nay, nay; lest ye fall into condemnation" (James 5:12).

Again, the word "but" is the little Greek word *de*, which is an exclamatory marker. It's the equivalent of James saying, "*Categorically* and *emphatically*, let your yea be yea and your nay, nay." The words "yea be yea and your nay, nay" means let your *Yes mean yes* and your *No mean no*. In other words, stay out of the retribution and revenge business. That's God's business, not yours.

Avoid Self-Inflicted Crises by Refusing To Settle the Score

If we take matters into our own hands, James said, "…Ye fall into condemnation" (James 5:12). In Greek, the words "ye fall" are from the word *pipto*, meaning *to fall*. It depicts *a downward plummet* or *one who falls into a terrible predicament or into a worse state than he was in before*. This word pictures *someone who falls into some type of failure*.

The word "into" here is a poor translation of the Greek word *hupo*, which would better be translated as *under*. When a person chooses to settle the score on his own, the Bible says he falls under "condemnation," which is the Greek word *krisis*. It is from where we get the word *crisis*, as in a *crisis situation*. This word *krisis* can describe *judgment by others* or *self-inflicted judgment*. It pictures *one who makes matters worse and creates a worse crisis*; hence, *self-inflicted troubles*.

So rather than make a bunch of threatening statements and say, "I'm tired of this injustice and I'm going to settle the score myself," James tells us to consider the story of Job and the prophets of old and study how they got through their hard times. In each case, they developed endurance — they kept their eyes fixed on the Lord and looked for His tender mercies to manifest in their lives. As a result, He acted on their behalf, and that's what the Lord will do in your life also if you'll stay in faith and keep a right attitude.

In our next lesson, we will zero in on what James had to say about the power of praying for one another.

STUDY QUESTIONS

Study to shew thyself approved unto God, a workman that needeth not to be ashamed, rightly dividing the word of truth.
— 2 Timothy 2:15

1. According to James 5:10, we can develop endurance for tough times by studying the prophets who lived before us. Which person from Scripture really encourages you and helps build your faith? What is it about their life that inspires you? Take some time to read through the details of their story. What can you learn from their example and apply in your life?
2. To understand the intensity of what Job experienced, read what happened to him in Job 1:1-22 and 2:1-10. What exactly did he lose? After so much tragedy, what did God do to bless Job? (*Hint*: Read Job: 42:10-17 to find out.)

3. The Greek word for "endure" is *hupomeno*, and the word translated "patience" is *hupomone* — both have the same meaning. Take a few moments to reread the meaning. What new insights are you seeing about this greatly needed virtue? What experiences has the Lord used in your life to help you develop endurance?

PRACTICAL APPLICATION

> But be ye doers of the word, and not hearers only,
> deceiving your own selves.
> —James 1:22

1. Did you know that God is deeply moved by everything you go through in life — so much so that He literally feels every bit of your pain? Think back for a minute to a situation that hurt you in the past. Have you talked to Him about it yet? Even though He already knows, letting out exactly how you feel is the first step toward healing, and one He can't wait for you to take.

2. How does knowing God cares and is moved by your pain change your view of Him and His involvement in your life? (Read these encouraging promises in Psalm 34:15-20; 56:8.)

3. When we make inner vows, we take the problems we're dealing with out of God's hands and put them back into ours, which never ends well. As much as we want to fix and control things, we just can't bring about the solutions that only God can. Is there an area of your life where you're tempted to take matters into your own hands? If so, where?

4. Have you ever promised yourself, "I'll never _____ again"? Which words complete that sentence for you? Whatever they are, they show you an area of your life where you've been disappointed, angered or hurt deeply, and ultimately what you're afraid of. Take a moment to pray something like this:

Lord, what pain or fear(s) has prompted me to make this vow? Please heal me from the heartache that drove me to make this promise, forgive me for trying to play Your role in my life, and help me release the fear that has been calling the shots. You are God and I am not. I need You to be God in my life, because You genuinely know what's best; You truly love me, and Your grace is what empowers me to change. Thank You for helping me let go of these inner promises and trust You to take care of me. In Jesus' name. Amen.

LESSON 4

TOPIC
Praying for Each Other

SCRIPTURES
1. **James 5:13-18** — Is any among you afflicted? let him pray. Is any merry? let him sing psalms. Is any sick among you? let him call for the elders of the church; and let them pray over him, anointing him with oil in the name of the Lord: And the prayer of faith shall save the sick, and the Lord shall raise him up; and if he have committed sins, they shall be forgiven him. Confess your faults one to another, and pray one for another, that ye may be healed. The effectual fervent prayer of a righteous man availeth much. Elias was a man subject to like passions as we are, and he prayed earnestly that it might not rain: and it rained not on the earth by the space of three years and six months. And he prayed again, and the heaven gave rain, and the earth brought forth her fruit.

GREEK WORDS
1. "afflicted" — κακοπαθέω (*kakopatheo*): to suffer evil; denotes something hurtful or damaging, such as the personal devastation that results from one's physical illness or evil circumstances; can picture a physical suffering or a suffering that occurs in the mind
2. "merry" — εὐθυμέω (*euthumeo*): a compound of the Greek words εὐ (*eu*) and θυμός (*thumos*); εὐ (*eu*) describes a good feeling, and it is where we get the word euphoric; pictures one who is elated, thrilled, or ecstatic about something; the word θυμός (*thumos*) is the idea of swelling emotions or a strong and growing passion about something; when these two are joined together to form the word εὐθυμέω (*euthumeo*) the new word expresses the idea of a person who is just about to explode with joy; one so excited and overjoyed that he can

hardly contain himself; he is so tickled about something that he can no longer restrain the happiness he feels

3. "sing psalms" — ψάλλω (*psallo*): to pluck, as to pluck the strings of a harp or bow; to play, as a musician would play a stringed instrument; by the time of the New Testament, it pictured a person who sings a hymn or some other special heartfelt expression of music

4. "sick" — ἀσθενέω (*astheneo*): a word that generally describes a person who is frail in health; people so physically weak that they were unable to travel; it carries the idea of those who were feeble, fragile, faint, incapacitated, disabled, or simply in such poor health that it would be unthinkable to transport them; shut-ins or homebound; can also mean to be in financial need

5. "call" — προσκαλέω (*proskaleo*): a compound of the words πρός (*pros*) and καλέω (*kaleo*); πρός (*pros*) means toward, and the word καλέω (*kaleo*); means to call, to invite, or to beckon; when compounded, to call, invite, or beckon; to summon to one's side

6. "elders" — πρεσβύτερος (*presbuteros*): used to depict the spiritual representatives of Israel, such as ruling members of local synagogues or teachers of the Law who publicly taught in synagogues; officially appointed church leaders

7. "anointing…with oil" — ἀλείφω (*aleipho*): the outward anointing of the body

8. "in the name" — ὄνομα (*onoma*): represents the full authority that exists in the person being named

9. "save" — σώζω (*sodzo*): to heal, but also conveys the idea of wholeness or salvation; delivering and healing power that results in wholeness; to deliver from enemies; to protect, keep safe, to keep under protection

10. "sick" — κάμνω (*kamno*): referring to a person who has long suffered from this affliction and is extremely weakened from the effects of this disease

11. "raise him up" — ἐγείρω (*egeiro*): to raise, and also the root from which we get the word resurrection

12. "sins" — ἁμαρτία (*hamartia*): to miss the mark; a failure; a fault

13. "forgiven" — ἀφίημι (*aphiemi*): to forgive: to release; to set free; to let go; to discharge; to send away

14. "confess" — εξομολογέω (*exomologeo*): a word that means to declare, to say out loud, to exclaim, to divulge, or to blurt

15. "faults" — ἁμαρτία (*hamartia*): to fall short; to miss the mark; one who habitually misses the mark and falls short of what God expects and approves
16. "one to another" — ἀλλήλων (*allelon*): each other; reciprocally; of each other
17. "that" — ὅπως (*hopos*): so that
18. "healed" — ἰάομαι (*iaomai*): to cure; to be doctored; mostly denoted healing that came to pass over a period of time
19. "effectual" — ἐνεργέω (*energeo*): energetic; depicts a powerful force that is ready to be set into motion; active and energetic
20. "prayer" — δέησις (*deisis*): a request for a concrete, specific need, usually some type of physical or material need, to be met; a request for a physical, tangible need to be met or supplied; a petition to meet a specific need that the person praying is facing in his life
21. "righteous man" — δίκαιος (*dikaios*): right; righteous; approved
22. "availeth much" — πολὺ ἰσχύει (*polu ishcuei*): has much ability and strength
23. "subject to like passions" — ὁμοιοπαθὴς ἡμῖν (*homoiopathes hemin*): similar struggles to us

SYNOPSIS

James 5:13-18 continued addressing the practical, relevant concerns of life — this time focusing on key issues such as advice for those dealing with devastating circumstances, prayer for the sick, and personal ministry to those homebound by long-term sickness. James also explained the importance and the restorative power of confessing our faults to those we trust and how our heartfelt, sincere prayers release God's supernatural strength to work in our lives. Are you ready? Let's dive into another action-packed lesson from the book of James!

The emphasis of this lesson:

The best thing a person can do who's suffering physically, mentally, and emotionally is to personally pray. If someone is feeling great about their life, they should sing songs of praise, and if someone is frail and homebound by sickness, they should call for their church leaders to come pray for them and anoint them with oil. The prayer of faith releases

delivering and healing power that results in wholeness in every area of one's life.

As we have seen, James was a master at packing a ton of down-to-earth instruction in a handful of verses. We see this once again in **James 5:13-18**, where he wrote:

> Is any among you afflicted? let him pray. Is any merry? let him sing psalms.
>
> Is any sick among you? let him call for the elders of the church; and let them pray over him, anointing him with oil in the name of the Lord:
>
> And the prayer of faith shall save the sick, and the Lord shall raise him up; and if he have committed sins, they shall be forgiven him.
>
> Confess your faults one to another, and pray one for another, that ye may be healed. The effectual fervent prayer of a righteous man availeth much.
>
> [Elijah] was a man subject to like passions as we are, and he prayed earnestly that it might not rain: and it rained not on the earth by the space of three years and six months.
>
> And he prayed again, and the heaven gave rain, and the earth brought forth her fruit.

To grasp the fullness of what the Holy Spirit is communicating through James, let's look at several of the key words in these verses and their meaning from the original Greek text.

What Does It Mean To Be 'Afflicted'?

Looking at James 5:13, he asked, "Is any among you afflicted? let him pray...." The word "afflicted" in this verse is very important. It is the Greek word *kakopatheo*, which is a compound of the words *kakos* and the word *pathos*. The word *kakos* describes something *foul, vile, horrible*, or *destructive*; and the word *pathos* denotes *a type of mental or emotional suffering*. When these words are compounded to form *kakopatheo*, it means *to suffer evil*. It denotes *something hurtful or damaging*, such as the personal devastation that results from one's physical illness or evil circumstances. It can also picture a physical suffering or a suffering that occurs in the mind.

Clearly, with all that had resulted from the Roman persecution and being scattered abroad, James' readers had endured various levels of physical suffering, and with it also came mental and emotional misery. To anyone who was facing such pain, James plainly said, "…Let him pray…" (James 5:13).

Notice he didn't say, "Ask a bunch of other Christians to pray for you." Instead, the responsibility of prayer first belongs to the person going through the hard time. Oftentimes when we have problems, we go to people instead of Jesus for help, and while it's good and helpful — even biblical — to have people join in agreement to pray over us, we first need to pray for ourselves.

Taking into account the original Greek meaning, here is the *Renner Interpretive Version (RIV)* of the first part of James 5:13:

> **Is anyone among you going through an extremely difficult time in life that is causing him a lot of grief? I urge that person to draw near to God, to pour his heart out to Him, and to be willing to give up anything and to do anything God requires in order for his situation to be changed.**

What Should You Do When You're Happy?

The second part of James 5:13 focuses on the opposite condition. James added, "…Is any merry? let him sing psalms." The two important words to understand in this verse are *merry* and *psalms*. The word "merry" is the Greek word *euthumeo*, which is a compound of the words *eu* and *thumos*. The little word *eu* describes *a good feeling*, and it's where we get the word *euphoric*. It pictures *one who is elated, thrilled, or ecstatic about something*. The word *thumos* is the idea of *swelling emotions* or *a strong and growing passion about something*. When these two words are joined together to form the new word *euthumeo*, it expresses the idea of *a person who is just about to explode with joy*. It is *one so excited and overjoyed that he can hardly contain himself*. He is so tickled about something that he can no longer restrain the happiness he feels.

Essentially, James said, "If you're elated, thrilled, and euphoric about all the great things going on in your life, *sing psalms*." The words "sing psalms" are a translation of the Greek word *psallo*, which means *to pluck*, as *to pluck the strings of a harp or bow*. It is the picture of a musician playing a stringed instrument. By the time of the New Testament, this word *psallo* pictured a person who sings a hymn or some other special heartfelt expression of music.

Therefore, when James said, "Sing psalms," it was the equivalent of him saying, "Grab your guitar and begin to rejoice!" Figuratively, this depicts a person plucking the "strings of their heart" as they begin to worship and sing to God. This verse lets us know that we don't have to wait for someone else to rejoice with us when something good happens. Instead, we can make a joyful noise to the Lord whenever and wherever we are.

Taking into account the original Greek meaning, here is the *Renner Interpretive Version (RIV)* of the second part of James 5:13:

Is there anyone among you so excited that he can hardly contain it and who feels as if he is about to burst with joy? If that person is so overjoyed and tickled that he can no longer restrain the happiness he feels, let him sing the song he feels in his heart.

Although you may initially burst into songs of worship alone, before you know it, God Himself will be there with you. The Bible says He "inhabits" the praises of His people — which means He is *magnetically drawn to and sits enthroned upon* those who worship Him.

How Is a Sick Person To Respond?

The next group of people James addresses is those that are *sick*. To them he said, "Is any sick among you? let him call for the elders of the church; and let them pray over him, anointing him with oil in the name of the Lord" (James 5:14). Now the reason he even asked this question was because these First-Century believers had learned that both physical healing and forgiveness of sin were provided through the atoning death and resurrection of Jesus. In their culture and time, few people ever mentioned when they were sick.

In the Greek, this word "sick" is *astheneo* — a word that generally describes *a person who is frail in health and so physically weak they are unable to travel*. It carries the idea of those who were *feeble, fragile, faint, incapacitated, disabled, or simply in such poor health that it would be unthinkable to transport them*. Hence, this word "sick" (*astheneo*) depicts *shut-ins* or those who are *homebound*. Moreover, it can also describe *people who are in financial need*, which makes sense because when your body is under physical attack and you're sick, you tend to spend a great deal of money to get well.

The point here is that those who are "sick" are very *frail*. They're not dealing with minor ailments like the common cold, a mild headache, or a stomachache. Their condition is so severe they are unable to travel to church to receive prayer. That is why James said, "Is any sick among you? let him call for the elders of the church; and let them pray over him, anointing him with oil in the name of the Lord" (James 5:14).

Call for the 'Elders' of the Church To Come Pray

Anyone who is this incapacitated by sickness is to *call* for the elders of the church to come to them. The word "call" is the Greek word *proskaleo*, which is a compound of the words *pros* and *kaleo*. The word *pros* means *toward*, and the word *kaleo* means *to call, to invite*, or *to beckon*. When these words are compounded, the new word *proskaleo* means *to call, invite*, or *beckon; to summon to one's side*. And the tense that is used here indicates an urgent plea requesting that the elders come and pray.

The Greek word for "elders" here is *presbuteros*, which was used to depict *the spiritual representatives of Israel*, such as ruling members of local synagogues or teachers of the Law who publicly taught in synagogues. In New Testament times, the word *presbuteros* (elders) described *officially appointed church leaders*. When a person was homebound by sickness, they were to get word to the official church leaders and request that they come to pray and anoint them with oil.

The phrase "anointing him with oil" is a translation of the Greek word *aleipho*, which simply describes *the outward anointing of the body with oil*. Although the oil itself has no healing properties, in both the Old and the New Testament it symbolically depicted the presence of the Holy Spirit and the power of God. The moment the oil is applied in a time of prayer is the moment the sick person is to release their faith for Christ's healing to manifest in their body.

This is a point of supernatural contact — the moment in which church leaders are to pray "…in the name of the Lord" (James 5:14). In Greek, the phrase "in the name" is a translation of the word *onoma*, and it represents *the full authority that exists in the person being named*.

Praying the Prayer of Faith 'in the Name of Jesus'

This means when we as believers pray "in Jesus' name," we actually stand in the physical place of Jesus and act on His behalf. Jesus has invested His authority into us to be His official representatives. Although He's seated at the right hand of the Father in Heaven, when we stand by the bedside of someone who's sick and pray "in Jesus' name" (*onoma*), Jesus is present because we are standing there on His behalf.

Think about it: What would Jesus do if He were physically present with someone sick? He would heal that person, right? That's why James goes on to say:

> **And the prayer of faith shall save the sick, and the Lord shall raise him up; and if he have committed sins, they shall be forgiven him.**
> —James 5:15

The Greek word for "save" in this verse is *sodzo*, which means *to save*, but also means *to heal* and conveys the idea of *wholeness* in every area of one's life. It is delivering and healing power that results in wholeness. Moreover, this word *sodzo* means *to deliver from one's enemies; to protect, keep safe*, and *to keep under protection*.

What's interesting is that the word "sick" here is different than in verse 14. It is the Greek word *kamno*, referring *to a person who has long suffered from this affliction and is extremely weakened from the effects of this disease*. When the prayer of faith is prayed and this sick person is anointed with oil in Jesus' name, the Bible says, "…The prayer of faith shall save the sick, and the Lord shall raise him up…" (James 5:15).

In Greek, the phrase "raise him up" is *egeiro*, which means *to raise* and is also the root from where we get the word *resurrection*. Thus, the person who has been suffering a long time from the effects of disease will be *raised out of their debilitating situation*. They were so sick and so close to death at the time they were prayed for that their recovery will appear to be *a resurrection*.

Taking into account the original Greek meanings, here is the *Renner Interpretive Version (RIV)* of James 5:14 and the first part of verse 15:

> **Is there anyone among you who is extremely weakened due to illness? If there is such a person, let him urgently call for the**

ordained leaders of the local assembly to come and passionately petition God on his behalf. As the leaders pray, let them also anoint the sick person with oil, standing in the very place of Jesus — acting on Jesus' behalf and using the authority of His Name. The prayer offered in faith will have definite results, for it will restore the sick person's health as the Lord raises him up from his bed of affliction.

Forgiveness and Healing Go Hand in Hand

James wraps up verse 15 by saying, "…And if he have committed sins, they shall be forgiven him" (James 5:15). The word "sins" is the plural form of the Greek word *hamartia*, which means *to miss the mark or fall short*. The implication here is that this person may have brought this severe sickness on themselves as a result of a repeated failure or fault. Even if this is the case, James says their sins "…shall be forgiven him" (James 5:15).

The word "forgiven" is the Greek word *aphiemi*, which means *to forgive* or *to release*. It is the idea of *setting free*, *letting go*, *discharging*, or *sending away permanently*. To all this James added these further instructions:

> **Confess your faults one to another, and pray one for another, that ye may be healed. The effectual fervent prayer of a righteous man availeth much.**
> —**James 5:16**

The word "confess" in Greek is *exomologeo*, a word that means *to declare*, *to say out loud*, *to exclaim*, *to divulge*, or *to blurt out*. Oftentimes when we've been trapped in a rut of wrong thinking and/or behavior, we're also full of shame, guilt, and condemnation. Yet, when we're in a safe place and talking to believers we trust, we don't have to be afraid or ashamed. We can be open and honest about our faults, temptations, and struggles, knowing they won't judge us, but will pray for and support us.

In Greek, the word "faults" is a form of the word *hamartia*, which is translated as "sins" in verse 15. Again, it means *to fall short* or *to miss the mark*. It depicts *one who habitually misses the mark and falls short of what God expects and approves*. To experience the wholeness Jesus died to give us, we have to begin the process by being honest with God, ourselves, and other believers we're close to and trust.

James said we need to declare or share our recurring failures "…one to another, and pray one for another…" (James 5:16). The phrase "one to another" is a translation of the Greek word *allelon*, and it means *each other* or *of each other*. It is action done *reciprocally*. The reason we confess our faults and pray for one another is so "…that [we] may be healed" (James 5:16).

The word "that" — the Greek word *hopos* — means *so that* and points to something explicit. We confess to and pray for one another *so that* we may be "healed." This word "healed" is very important. It is the Greek word *iaomai*, which means *to cure* or *to be doctored*. This word primarily denoted *healing that came to pass over a period of time*; not instantaneously. Very often, that's how deliverance and healing takes place in our lives — gradually. This healing begins and is set in motion the moment we begin to admit and blurt out our faults to a trusted friend. Then step by step, we experience freedom.

The Dynamic Power of a Heartfelt Prayer

Amazingly, when the first part of James 5:16 is implemented, the second part of verse 16 is activated. The Bible says, "…The effectual fervent prayer of a righteous man availeth much" (James 5:16). The word "effectual" is the Greek word *energeo*, and it means *energetic*. It depicts *a powerful force that is ready to be set into motion; something active, energetic, and filled with divine power*.

This brings us to the word "prayer," which is the Greek word *deisis*. It describes *a request for a concrete, specific need, usually some type of physical or material need, to be met*. It is *a request for a physical, tangible need to be met or supplied*. This is not a general, "Bless me Lord" prayer — it's a petition to meet a specific need that the person praying is facing in his life.

James said, "…The effectual fervent prayer of a righteous man availeth much" (James 5:16). The words "righteous man" is the Greek word *dikaios*, which means *right; righteous;* and *approved*. This is the condition of every person who has repented of their sin, received Jesus' sacrifice for them, and asked Him to be their Lord and Savior. The moment we surrender our lives to Jesus, God calls us *righteous*, and our prayers "availeth much," which literally means they *have much ability and strength*.

To make sure we realize that our prayers are just as powerful as anyone else in Scripture, James gave us this example of the prophet Elijah:

> **[Elijah] was a man subject to like passions as we are, and he prayed earnestly that it might not rain: and it rained not on the earth by the space of three years and six months. And he prayed again, and the heaven gave rain, and the earth brought forth her fruit.**
> — **James 5:17,18**

The phrase "subject to like passions" in Greek simply means *having similar struggles to us*. Elijah struggled with many of the same issues we face today, but those struggles didn't disqualify him from being used in amazing ways by God — neither do they disqualify you! You are the righteousness of God in Christ (*see* 2 Corinthians 5:21), and the same Holy Spirit that raised Jesus from the dead lives in you (*see* Romans 8:11). This means that when you obey the instructions in James 5:16, your prayers will also release God's strength and ability!

In our final lesson, we will focus on how to respond when a loved one or friend has veered from the faith and greatly messed up their life.

STUDY QUESTIONS

> **Study to shew thyself approved unto God, a workman that needeth not to be ashamed, rightly dividing the word of truth.**
> — 2 Timothy 2:15

1. The Bible says, "…The earnest (heartfelt, continued) prayer of a righteous man makes tremendous power available [dynamic in its working]" (James 5:16 *AMPC*). What stories come to mind from God's Word when you think of the power of sincere, believing prayer? Consider these examples:
   - Gideon's Prayer (Judges 6:36-40)
   - Hannah's Prayer (1 Samuel 1 and 2)
   - The Prayer of Jabez (1 Chronicles 4:9,10)
   - The Disciples' and the Church's Prayer (Acts 12:5-17)
   - Jesus' Prayer (John 11:41-44)

2. James 5:13 (*NIV*) says, "…Is anyone happy? Let them sing songs of praise." What connection can you see between James' instruction and the words of Paul in Ephesians 5:19,20 and Colossians 3:16? Accord-

ing to these verses and Psalm 100, what can you begin doing regularly to stir up and maintain a desire to praise God?

3. Take a few moments to review the definition of the word "afflicted." In light of its meaning, what is *afflicting* you right now? Pray and invite the Holy Spirit to bring the *freedom* and *wholeness* to your life that only He can bring — and to show you what steps you can take to participate in the process of healing.

PRACTICAL APPLICATION

> But be ye doers of the word, and not hearers only, deceiving your own selves.
> — James 1:22

We can and should share our faults, struggles, and challenges with sin with believers we trust so they can pray for us and lovingly hold us accountable. When we cultivate an environment of trust, vulnerability, and love, we can confess our sins to each other without fear and experience the freedom and wholeness God wants for us.

1. Do you have anyone in your life you can be honest with on this level? If so, how can you begin to create time and space for these hard-but-needed conversations? If not, ask God to direct your steps and provide a divine connection with the right people with whom you can be real and do life with.

2. Can you remember a time when confessing something — good or bad — helped you feel less alone? What did you share and how did talking with someone positively impact your life? What aspect of your life or personality do you feel God is nudging you to bring into the light?

LESSON 5

TOPIC
Hiding a Multitude of Sins

SCRIPTURES
1. **James 5:16-20** — Confess your faults one to another, and pray one for another, that ye may be healed. The effectual fervent prayer of a righteous man availeth much. Elias was a man subject to like passions as we are, and he prayed earnestly that it might not rain: and it rained not on the earth by the space of three years and six months. And he prayed again, and the heaven gave rain, and the earth brought forth her fruit. Brethren, if any of you do err from the truth, and one convert him; Let him know, that he which converteth the sinner from the error of his way shall save a soul from death, and shall hide a multitude of sins.

GREEK WORDS
1. "effectual" — ἐνεργέω (*energeo*): energetic; depicts a powerful force that is ready to be set into motion; active and energetic
2. "prayer" — δέησις (*deisis*): a request for a concrete, specific need, usually some type of physical or material need, to be met; a request for a physical, tangible need to be met or supplied; a petition to meet a specific need that the person praying is facing in his life
3. "righteous man" — δίκαιος (*dikaios*): right; righteous; approved
4. "availeth much" — πολὺ ἰσχύει (*polu ishcuei*): has much ability and strength
5. "subject to like passions" — ὁμοιοπαθὴς ἡμῖν (*homoiopathes hemin*): similar struggles to us
6. "brethren" — ἀδελφός (*adelphos*): a term used to describe two or more who were born from the same womb; an endearing term used to describe those of one's own family; later used in a military sense to depict brothers in battle; a comrade; hence, brotherhood
7. "if" — ἐάν (*ean*): the idea of a certain possibility; in all likelihood, it probably will happen
8. "any of you" — τις ἐν ὑμῖν (*tis en humin*): anyone in your midst

9. "err" — **πλανάω** (*planao*): deception; a moral wandering; it depicts a person who has veered from a solid path; as a result of veering morally, they are adrift; used to depict a lost animal that cannot find its path; to morally lose one's bearings
10. "from" — **ἀπό** (*apo*): away from; implies putting distance between oneself and something else
11. "the truth" — **τῆς ἀληθείας** (*tes aletheias*): a definite article with **ἀλήθεια** (*aletheia*); THE truth as revealed in Scripture
12. "convert" — **ἐπιστρέφω** (*epistrepho*): a turning point; to turn around; to turn back; to return
13. "know" — **γινώσκω** (*ginosko*): realize; pictures a full comprehension
14. "converteth" — **ἐπιστρέφω** (*epistrepho*): a turning point; to turn around; to turn back; to return
15. "sinner" — **ἁμαρτωλός** (*hamartolos*): one who habitually misses the mark and falls short of what God expects and approves
16. "from" — **ἐκ** (*ek*): out of
17. "error" — **πλανάω** (*planao*): deception; a moral wandering; depicts one who has veered from a solid path; as a result of veering morally, he is adrift; depicts a lost animal that cannot find its path; to morally lose one's bearings
18. "way" — **ὁδός** (*hodos*): way; roads upon which one travels
19. "save" — **σῴζω** (*sodzo*): to heal, but also conveys the idea of wholeness or salvation; delivering and healing power that results in wholeness; to deliver from enemies; to protect, keep safe, to keep under protection
20. "from death" — **ἐκ θανάτου** (*ek thanatou*): from death; **θάνατος** (*thanatos*) can be physical or spiritual death, mortal danger, or a dangerous circumstance; a death sentence
21. "hide" — **καλύπτω** (*kalupto*): conceal; cover; veil; hide from view
22. "multitude of sins" — **πλῆθος ἁμαρτιῶν** (*plethos harmartion*): picturing fullness of sins

SYNOPSIS

Our study on the book of James has proven to be an amazing journey, and this final lesson is just as remarkable. In the two closing verses of Chapter 5, James talks about the importance of reaching out to help backslidden believers return to the Lord. In light of Jesus' warning of the great deception in the last days and Paul's prophecy of a departure from the faith, James advises us to help those who "err from the truth" come to their senses and save their soul from death.

The emphasis of this lesson:
In these last of the last days, it's very likely that you'll come across believers who have *erred* from the truth. Little by little, they have swallowed the enemy's devilish deception and wandered off the solid path of truth they once walked on. God wants us to help these erring individuals turn back to Him and repent. Every soul we help save is delivered from a death sentence and kept safe under God's protection.

You Are Righteous In Christ and Your Prayers Are Powerful!

As we wrapped up Lesson 4, we learned about the dynamic power that is released when we pray. James 5:16 says, "…The effectual fervent prayer of a righteous man availeth much." Now if you read that verse and think, *Well, that doesn't include me because I'm not righteous*, there's good news for you. Although you may not *feel* righteous or *behave* in a way you think will make you righteous, it doesn't change the fact that in Christ, you ARE righteous! The apostle Paul makes this explicitly clear in the *Amplified* version of Second Corinthians 5:21:

> **For our sake He [God] made Christ [virtually] to be sin Who knew no sin, so that in and through Him we might become [endued with, viewed as being in, and examples of] the righteousness of God [what we ought to be, approved and acceptable and in right relationship with Him, by His goodness].**

As a born-again Christ-follower, being **righteous** is both your spiritual condition *and* position in Jesus. It has nothing to do with how you feel or what you've done and everything to do with what Jesus did. The moment you repented of your sins and made Him the Lord of your life, His Blood washed away your sins and you were forgiven. In that instant, God the Father imputed — which means He *credited*, *assigned*, or *ascribed* — righteousness to you (*see* Romans 4:5,6).

The Greek word for "righteous" in James 5:16 is *dikaios*, which means *right*, *righteous*, and *approved*. As a righteous person, your prayers are *effectual* and avail much. The word "effectual" in this verse is the Greek word *energeo*, which is where we get the word *energy*. It depicts something *energetic* or *active*. It is *a powerful force that is ready to be set into motion*. This is James' description of our prayers.

Now the Greek word for "prayer" here is very distinct. It is the word *deisis*, which describes *a request for a concrete, specific need, usually some type of physical or material need, to be met*. It is *a request for a physical, tangible need to be met or supplied*; *a petition to meet a specific need that the person praying is facing in his life*. The fact that this word *deisis* is used here tells us that God wants us to be very specific when we pray. If we want *specific results*, we need to pray and make *specific requests*, and when we do, our prayers will "availeth much."

In Greek, the phrase "availeth much" literally means *has much ability and strength*. In fact, the word *strength* that is used here is from the Greek word *ishchuos*, which describes a mighty man like a bodybuilder whose arms are strapping and bulging with muscles. Just one flex of muscle and he can release tremendous power. The implication here is that when we pray in the name of Jesus, great power is released into our lives and the situations we're facing. That's what "availeth much" — translated from the Greek words *polu ishcuei* — means.

If God Could Use Elijah, He Can Use You

Of all the Old Testament prophets, Elijah is certainly celebrated as one of the greatest to ever live. Interestingly, James uses him as an example of what our prayers can produce, saying, "[Elijah] was a man subject to like passions as we are, and he prayed earnestly that it might not rain: and it rained not on the earth by the space of three years and six months" (James 5:17).

A key to understanding this verse is in identifying the meaning of the phrase "subject to like passions." In Greek, it simply means Elijah *had similar struggles as we do*. A careful evaluation of his life reveals his great zeal and passion for God along with his bouts with fear and depression. It is important to see his humanness — which is what James is subtly pointing to — because it helps us understand that God really can use anyone to do great things.

James said, "…[Elijah] prayed earnestly that it might not rain: and it rained not on the earth by the space of three years and six months. And he prayed again, and the heaven gave rain, and the earth brought forth her fruit (James 5:17,18). In spite of his vacillating faith, Elijah was highly effective when he prayed. So if it seems like one day you're spiritually on top of a mountain and the next day you're in a valley of depression, you're in good company. That is the story of Elijah's life. And if God could use him, He can certainly use you too!

James Called His Readers 'Brethren' Sixteen Times

James concludes his letter by saying: "Brethren, if any of you do err from the truth, and one convert him; Let him know, that he which converteth the sinner from the error of his way shall save a soul from death, and shall hide a multitude of sins" (James 5:19,20).

First of all, notice that James begins verse 19 by calling his readers "brethren" once again. This is the sixteenth time in five chapters that he uses the same Greek word, the word *adelphos*. It is derived from the word *delphos*, which describes *the womb of a woman*, but when an "a" is placed on the front of it, the condition is reversed. Hence, it signifies *one born out of a womb*.

In this case, because it is the word for "brother," it means *two or more born out of the same womb*. James uses this word to describe fellow believers that are all born out of the womb of God. This very endearing term was initially used to describe those of one's own family, and it was later used in a military sense to depict *brothers in battle*; *camaraderie*; or *a brotherhood*.

Keep in mind the person using this word is James — the half-brother of Jesus and great, legendary leader of the church in Jerusalem. At that time, he was the most visible and influential frontrunner in the Church. Believers who had been scattered all across the eastern lands of the Roman Empire had written to him seeking help and advice regarding the overwhelming challenges they were facing. Rather than speak down to them, James called them "brethren" (*adelphos*) sixteen times, and by doing so he symbolically got down into the trenches with his readers and identified himself as one of them.

Essentially, he said, "I'm proud to be your fellow soldier! We're comrades together — real brothers in Christ." Likewise, you too may know someone who's struggling in their faith and asking many questions. But as long as they're still trying and they haven't given up, you need to come alongside them and say, "I'm proud to be your brother/sister in Christ! It's a privilege to be in God's family with you."

What Does It Mean To 'Err' from the Truth?

Looking once more at verse 19, James said, "Brethren, if any of you do err from the truth…" (James 5:19). The word "if" in Greek here is *ean*, and it conveys *the idea of a certain possibility* and means *in all likelihood, it probably will happen*. The phrase "any of you," translated from the Greek words *tis en humin*, indicates *anyone in your midst*. In context here, James is saying, "In all likelihood, there's a strong possibility that you will come across someone you know who *errs* from the truth."

This brings us to the word "err," which is a translation of the very important Greek word *planao*. It is the very same word used by Jesus to describe the number one sign we would see just before He returns. The Bible says that as He sat upon the Mount of Olives, He gave this warning: "…Take heed that no man deceive you" (Matthew 24:4). The word "deceive" is the Greek word *planao* — the same word translated as "err" in James 5:19.

This word *planao* describes *a deception* or *a moral wandering*. It depicts *an individual, a group, or even a nation who has veered from a solid path they once walked on*. As a result of veering morally, they are adrift and no longer anchored to the truth. Jesus said this level of great deception will be the greatest sign to let us know that we have come to the very end of the age and His return is near.

The fact of the matter is, deception and error is all around us. It seems as though people in society are morally confused and have lost their minds. Right is called wrong, and wrong is called right and even celebrated in the streets. Indeed, the world around us is adrift and no longer anchored to the timeless truth of God's Word.

Paul Prophesied There Would Be a 'Departure From the Faith'

Interestingly, the apostle Paul prophesied that great deception would also take place in the Church. Under the inspiration of the Holy Spirit, the apostle Paul wrote, "Now the Spirit speaketh expressly, that in the latter times some shall depart from the faith, giving heed to seducing spirits, and doctrines of devils" (1 Timothy 4:1).

The period Paul notes for these events to occur are the "latter times." The word "latter" is the Greek word *husteros*, which describes *the ultimate end or the very last of something*. And the word "times" is the Greek word *kairos*, which describes *a season*. Together, *husteros kairos* — translated here as "latter times" — describes *the very last season or period of the Church age*. By using these words, the Holy Spirit gave us one of the major signs that we are living in the very end of the age.

Paul said, "…In the latter times, some shall depart from the faith…" (1 Timothy 4:1). The word "depart" in this verse is important. It is the Greek word *aphistemi*, which is a compound of the words *apo*, meaning *away*, and the word *histimi*, meaning *to stand*. When these words are compounded, they form the word *aphistemi*, which means *to stand apart from; to distance one's self from; to step away from; to withdraw from; or to shrink away from*. It is from this Greek word that we derive the words *apostate* and *apostasy*.

Now this *departure* is not an abrupt rejection of the faith. It is *a very gradual withdrawal* that takes place steadily over a period of time. It is the picture a person who slowly but surely changes the position of what he or she once believed. Instead of holding firmly to the faith, they begin to entertain other options and ideas that progressively lead them away from what they once believed. This departure is so gradual that those who are in the process of withdrawing may not even realize it is happening.

Specifically, the Bible says they will depart from "the faith." In Greek, this is the word *pisteos*, and it refers to *doctrine* or *to the long-held, time-tested teachings of Scripture*. What is interesting here is that it includes a definite article. In other words, this is not talking about a departure from faith in miracles or faith in healing per se. It is a slow drifting from "THE faith" — *the clear, timeless teaching of Scripture*.

All Deception Is Demonically Engineered

The Bible says the gradual drift away from the truth will result from people "…giving heed to seducing spirits, and doctrines of devils" (1 Timothy 4:1). In Greek, the words "giving heed" is the word *prosecho*, which is a compound of the word *pros*, meaning *to lean toward*, and the word *echo*, meaning *to embrace* or *to hold*. When these words are joined to form the word *prosecho*, it pictures *a person who has believed one thing for a very long time but is now leaning in a new direction, believing something else.* They have opened their mind to possibilities other than Scripture, and slowly but surely, they have withdrawn from what they once held precious and dear and have begun to grab hold of new ideas and new belief systems.

What is the energizing force behind this deception? Paul said, "…seducing spirits and doctrines of devils" (1 Timothy 4:1).

The word "doctrines" is the Greek word *didaskalia*, which describes *a well-packaged teaching that is applicable to a lifestyle.* Thus, when it's presented, the error sounds logical and appeals to one's flesh. And behind these well-packaged systems of thought that are being promoted are "devils." This is a translation of the Greek word *daimonion*, which in context, describes *evil spirits, demons, devils.* Now when the devil comes knocking on our door, he doesn't show up with horns on his head, a long tail, and a red pitchfork in his hand. Rather, he comes with the slickest PR infomercial ever produced, offering ideas that are tantalizing and mesmerizing in an effort to get you to accept his invitation and veer from the path of Scripture.

Paul also said we're dealing with *seducing spirits.* The word "seducing" in this verse is a translation of the Greek word *planao* — the same word translated as "err" in James 5:19. Again, it describes *deception* or a *moral wandering* and denotes *an individual, a group, or even a nation who has veered from a solid path that they once walked on.* As a result of slowly changing course morally, they are adrift and no longer anchored to the truth.

Again, James said that people would err "…from the truth…" (James 5:19). The word "from" is important. It is the Greek word *apo*, which means *away from* and implies *putting distance between oneself and something else.* In this case, these erring, deceived individuals are putting distance between themselves and "the truth," which in Greek is *tes aletheias.* It is a definite article with the word *aletheia*, meaning *THE truth as revealed in Scripture.*

God Wants Us to Help Erring Believers Turn Back to Him

Returning to James' closing words, he said, "Brethren, if any of you do err from the truth, and one convert him; Let him know, that he which converteth the sinner from the error of his way shall save a soul from death…"

(James 5:19,20). In the Greek, the words "convert" and "converteth" are a translation of the word *epistrepho*, which is a compound of the words *epi* and *strepho*. The word *epi* means *upon*, and the word *strepho*, describes *a turning point*. When these two words are compounded to form *epistrepho*, it means *to turn around*; *to turn back*; or *to return*.

When you help a believer who's veered off track to wake up and realize the error of their way and return home, it means that he or she repents and gets back on track with God. To anyone who helps someone in this way, James said, "…Know, that he which converteth the sinner from the error of his way shall save a soul from death…" (James 5:20). The word "know" here is a form of the Greek word *ginosko*, which means *to realize*, *to understand*, or *to fully comprehend*. God wants us to fully grasp the eternal difference we have made.

Who did James say we're to help? He used the word "sinner," which in Greek is *hamartolos* and describes *one who habitually misses the mark and falls short of what God expects and approves*. These are the individuals James said we're to help turn "from the error of their way." The word "from" here is the Greek word *ek*, which means *out of* and carries the idea of *deliverance*. The word "error" is again the Greek word *planao*, which describes *deception* or *a moral wandering* and depicts *one who has veered from a solid path he once walked upon*. And the word "way" is *hodos*, which is the Greek word for *a road*. In this case, it indicates *the wrong road* a sinner has been traveling on that is taking them away from God.

When you do something to help a backslidden believer return to God and get on the right road, James said, "…[You] shall save a soul from death, and shall hide a multitude of sins" (James 5:20). The word "save" here is the Greek word *sodzo*, which means *to heal*, but also conveys the idea of *wholeness* or *salvation*. It is *delivering and healing power that results in wholeness*. Furthermore, it means *to deliver from enemies*; *to protect*, *keep safe*, or *to keep under protection*.

Our Efforts Deliver Them From a Death Sentence

What are we saving them from? James said, "from death," which in Greek is *ek thanatou*. The word *ek* means *out*, and *thanatou* is from the word *thanatos*, which is the term for *death*. In this verse, it can depict *physical or spiritual death*, *mortal danger*, or *a dangerous circumstance*. It is the very word that was used by Greeks to describe *a death sentence*.

The truth is there are many believers who don't realize the slippery slope they are on or how dangerous the circumstances are that they're living in. When we help these individuals return to God and His Word, we save their soul from death. In other words, we deliver them from the death sentence pronounced on them by the enemy, bringing them back into a safe place where they're protected by God's Word and the power of the Holy Spirit.

In addition to delivering them from a death sentence, James said we "...shall hide a multitude of sins" (James 5:20). The word "hide" in Greek is *kalupto*, which means *to conceal, cover, veil*, or *hide from view*. And the Greek meaning of a "multitude of sins" pictures a fullness of sins. Regardless of what this person has done, if he or she repents and turns back to the Lord, all his sins will be cleansed by the blood of Jesus.

Friend, there is great joy in seeing a fellow believer who has lost their way return to God. The Bible says, "The fruit of the righteous is a tree of life, and the one who is wise saves lives" (Proverbs 11:30 *NIV*). God wants you to know — *to realize, to understand, to fully comprehend* — the eternal difference you're making through the power of your prayers and the example of your life. Keep up the great work — it pleases God immensely!

STUDY QUESTIONS

> **Study to shew thyself approved unto God, a workman that needeth not to be ashamed, rightly dividing the word of truth.**
> **— 2 Timothy 2:15**

1. Take a moment to reread James 5:19,20. How are the following passages related to what James said? What is the Holy Spirit speaking to you and showing you in these verses?
    - Romans 15:1,2 and 1 Thessalonians 5:14
    - 2 Timothy 2:24-26 and Jude 22,23
    - Proverbs 11:30 and Daniel 12:3

2. Remember what James said about Elijah? In spite of the fact that he struggled with fear, depression, and other very normal human challenges, his prayers still had dynamic power and God used him in unforgettable ways. How does his example change your view of what

God can do in and through *you* — especially in regard to helping the lost return to Him?
3. In addition to your prayers, the life you live is extremely impactful to those around you. Take time to reflect on this eye-opening principle from Proverbs. What is the Holy Spirit speaking to you through this passage about the example of your life?

He who heeds instruction and correction is [not only himself] in the way of life [but also] is a way of life for others. And he who neglects or refuses reproof [not only himself] goes astray [but also] causes to err and is a path toward ruin for others (Proverbs 10:17 *AMPC*).

PRACTICAL APPLICATION

> But be ye doers of the word, and not hearers only, deceiving your own selves.
> —James 1:22

1. The Bible consistently states that the closer we get to Jesus' return, the more people — both outside and inside the Church — would fall into deception. Can you remember a time when you were deceived about something? How did you realize you had veered off the right path? Who did the Lord use to speak into your life? What motivated you to turn around?
2. Do you know anyone who was pursuing Jesus and following His Word consistently, but they don't anymore? What can you learn from them or about their choices and the path they took away from Him that will help you avoid drifting in the same way?
3. Does this lesson ring a bell for you? Are you close to anyone who's wandered from the faith? What do you feel God is leading you to do about it? How can you specifically pray for them and release God's power to help save their soul from death?

Notes

Notes

CLAIM YOUR FREE RESOURCE!

As a way of introducing you further to the teaching ministry of Rick Renner, we would like to send you free of charge his teaching CD, "How To Receive a Miraculous Touch From God."

In His earthly ministry, Jesus commonly healed *all* who were sick of *all* their diseases. In this profound message, learn about the manifold dimensions of Christ's wisdom, goodness, power, and love toward all humanity who came to Him in faith with their needs.

☑ YES, I want to receive Rick Renner's monthly teaching letter!

Simply scan the QR code to claim this resource or go to:
renner.org/claim-your-free-offer

WITH US!

 renner.org    facebook.com/rickrenner

 youtube.com/rennerministries    instagram.com/rickrrenner

www.ingramcontent.com/pod-product-compliance
Lightning Source LLC
Chambersburg PA
CBHW061249040426
42444CB00010B/2307